THE AGPEYA
"Ϯⲁϫⲡⲓⲁ"

THE COPTIC PRAYER BOOK OF THE SEVEN HOURS

**Virgin Mary and Archangel Michael
Coptic Orthodox Church
of Connecticut, U.S.A.**
87 Benham Street, Hamden, CT 06514

The Agpeya
ϮⲀⲅⲡⲓⲁ

The Coptic Prayer Book of the Seven Hours

Edited by: Fr. Abraham Azmy
2020

ISBN: 9781712786253

Published by:

Virgin Mary and Archangel Michael Coptic Orthodox Church of Connecticut, U.S.A.
87 Benham Street
Hamden, CT 06514
T: (203) 248-5592
F: (203) 248-3898

www.coptnet.com

His Holiness Pope Tawadros II
Pope of Alexandria and
Patriarch of the See of St. Mark

His Grace Bishop David
Bishop of the Coptic Orthodox Diocese of
New York and New England

TABLE OF CONTENTS

INTRODUCTION TO EVERY HOUR

In the name of the Father, and the Son, and the Holy Spirit, one God. Amen.
Kyrie eleison. Lord have mercy, Lord have mercy, Lord bless us. Amen.
Glory to the Father, and to the Son, and to the Holy Spirit, now and forever and unto the ages of all ages. Amen.

THE LORD'S PRAYER

Make us worthy to pray thankfully:

Our Father Who art in heaven; hallowed be Thy name. Thy kingdom come. Thy will be done on earth as it is in heaven. Give us this day our daily bread. And forgive us our trespasses, as we forgive those who trespass against us. And lead us not into temptation, but deliver us from evil, in Christ Jesus our Lord. For Thine is the kingdom, the power and the glory, forever. Amen.

THE PRAYER OF THANKSGIVING

Let us give thanks to the beneficent and merciful God, the Father of our Lord, God and Savior, Jesus Christ, for He has covered us, helped us, guarded us, accepted us unto Him, spared us, supported us, and brought us to this hour. Let us also ask Him, the Lord our God, the Pantocrator (*Almighty*), to guard us in all peace this holy day and all the days of our life. O Master, Lord, God the Pantocrator (*Almighty*), the Father of our Lord, God and Savior, Jesus Christ, we thank You for every condition, concerning every condition, and in every condition, for You have covered us, helped us, guarded us, accepted us unto You, spared us, supported us, and brought us to this hour.

Therefore, we ask and entreat Your goodness, O Lover of mankind, to grant us to complete this holy day, and all the days of our life, in all peace with Your fear. All envy, all temptation, all the work of Satan, the counsel of wicked men, and the rising up of enemies, hidden and manifest, take them away from us, and from all Your people, and from this holy place that is Yours. But those things which are good and profitable do provide for us; for it is You Who have given us the authority to tread on serpents and scorpions, and upon all the power of the enemy. And lead us not into temptation, but deliver us from evil, by the grace, compassion and love of mankind, of Your Only-Begotten Son, our Lord, God and Savior, Jesus Christ, through Whom the glory, the honor, the dominion, and the adoration are due unto You, with Him, and the Holy Spirit, the Life-Giver, Who is of one essence with You, now and at all times, and unto the ages of all ages. Amen.

PSALM 50

Have mercy upon me, O God, according to Your great mercy; and according to the multitude of Your compassions blot out my iniquity. Wash me thoroughly from my iniquity, and cleanse me from my sin. For I am conscious of my iniquity; and my sin is at all times before me.
Against You only I have sinned, and done evil before You: that You might be just in Your sayings, and might overcome when You are judged. For, behold, I was conceived in iniquities, and in sins my mother conceived me. For, behold, You have loved the truth: You have manifested to me the hidden and unrevealed

things of Your wisdom. You shall sprinkle me with Your hyssop, and I shall be purified: You shall wash me, and I shall be made whiter than snow. You shall make me to hear gladness and joy: the humbled bones shall rejoice. Turn away Your face from my sins, and blot out all my iniquities. Create in me a clean heart, O God; and renew a right spirit in my inward parts. Do not cast me away from Your face; and do not remove Your Holy Spirit from me.

Give me the joy of Your salvation: and uphold me with a directing spirit. Then I shall teach the transgressors Your ways; and the ungodly men shall turn to You. Deliver me from blood, O God, the God of my salvation: and my tongue shall rejoice in Your righteousness.

O Lord, You shall open my lips; and my mouth shall declare Your praise. For if You desired sacrifice, I would have given it: You do not take pleasure in burnt offerings. The sacrifice of God is a broken spirit: a broken and humbled heart God shall not despise. Do good, O Lord, in Your good pleasure to Zion; and let the walls of Jerusalem be built. Then You shall be pleased with sacrifices of righteousness, offering, and burnt sacrifices: then they shall offer calves upon Your altar. **ALLELUIA.**

The First Hour – Prime

(It commemorates the hour at which our Lord Jesus Christ rose from the dead. It is prayed in the morning after rising up from sleep to glorify God in His resurrection and to thank Him for the beginning of a new day)

The Introduction of Every Hour:

The Lord's Prayer   **Page 1**
The Thanksgiving prayer   **Page 2**
Psalm 50   **Page 3**

Come let us kneel down, let us ask Christ our God. Come let us kneel down, let us beseech Christ our King. Come let us kneel down, let us entreat Christ our Savior. O Lord Jesus Christ, the Word of God, our God, through the intercession of Saint Mary and all Your saints, preserve us, and bring us to a good start. Have mercy on us according to Your will forever. The night has passed; we thank You, O Lord, and we ask You to keep us this day away from sin and deliver us.

THE PAULINE EPISTLE (Ephesians 4:1-5)

I, therefore, the prisoner of the Lord, beseech you to walk worthy of the calling with which you were called, with all lowliness and meekness, with longsuffering, bearing with one another in love, endeavoring to keep the unity of the Spirit in the bond of peace. There is one body, and one Spirit, just as you were called in one hope of your calling; one Lord, one faith, one baptism.

THE FAITH OF THE CHURCH

One is God the Father of everyone.

One is His Son, Jesus Christ the Word, Who took flesh and died; and rose from the dead on the third day, and raised us with Him.

One is the Holy Spirit, the Comforter, one in His Hypostasis, proceeding from the Father, purifying the whole creation, and teaching us to worship the Holy Trinity, one in divinity and one in essence. We praise Him and bless Him forever. Amen.

The Morning Prayer of the blessed day, we offer to Christ our King and our God, beseeching Him to forgive us our sins.
From the Psalms of our father David the prophet and the king, may his blessings be upon us all. Amen.

(1)　　　　**PSALM 1**

Blessed is the man who has not walked in the counsel of the ungodly, and has not stood in the way of the sinners, and has not sat in the seat of the evil men. But his will is in the law of the Lord; and in His law he shall meditate day and night. He shall be like the tree which is planted by the streams of water, which shall yield its fruit in its due season, and its leaf shall not scatter, and in everything he does he prospers. Not so are the ungodly, not so; but rather they are like the chaff which the wind scatters upon the face of the earth. Therefore the ungodly shall not stand in judgment, nor the sinners in the council of the righteous. For the Lord knows the way of the righteous; but the way of the ungodly shall perish. ALLELUIA.

(2)   **PSALM 2**

Why did the nations rage, and the peoples meditate on vain things? The kings of the earth stood up, and the rulers gathered together against the Lord and against His Christ; saying, "Let us break through their bonds, and cast away their yoke from us." He who dwells in the heavens shall laugh at them, and the Lord shall mock them. Then He shall speak to them in His anger, and in His wrath He shall trouble them. "But I have been established king by Him on Zion, His holy mountain, proclaiming the ordinance of the Lord: the Lord said to Me, `You are My Son, today I have begotten You. Ask Me, and I will give You the nations for Your inheritance, and Your authority to the end of the earth. You shall shepherd them with a rod of iron; You shall crush them as a potter's vessel." Now, understand, O kings: be instructed, all you who judge the earth, serve the Lord with fear, and rejoice in Him with trembling. Take hold of instruction, lest the Lord be angry, and you perish from the way of righteousness, whenever His wrath shall be suddenly kindled. Blessed are all who trust in Him. ALLELUIA.

(3)   **PSALM 3**

O Lord, why have they who afflict me multiplied? Many have risen up upon me. Many say unto my soul, "There is no salvation for him in his God." But You, O Lord, are my supporter, my glory, and the elevation of my head. With my voice I cried unto the Lord, and He heard me out of His holy mountain. I laid down and slept; and I arose; for the Lord is He who supports me. I will not be afraid of ten thousands of people, who surround me; who have risen upon me. Rise, O Lord, save me, O my God: for You have smitten all who are enemies to me without cause. The teeth of the sinners You have broken. Salvation is the Lord's, and His blessing is upon His people. ALLELUIA.

(4)   **PSALM 4**

When I cried out, God of my righteousness heard me: in tribulation You have made room for me; have compassion upon me, O Lord, and hear my prayer. O you, sons of men, how long will your hearts be heavy? Why do you love vanity, and seek falsehood? Know you that the Lord has made His Holy One wondrous. The Lord hears me when I cry to Him. Be angry, and do not sin; feel sorrow upon your beds for what you say in your hearts. Offer the sacrifice of righteousness, and trust in the Lord. Many say, "Who can show us the good things?" The light of Your countenance, O Lord, has been shined upon us. You have given gladness to my heart: they have been multiplied with the fruit of their wheat and wine and oil. I shall both lie down in peace and sleep: for You alone, O Lord, have caused me to dwell in hope. ALLELUIA.

(5) **PSALM 5**

Hearken, O Lord, to my words and consider my cry. Observe the voice of my supplication, my King, and my God: for to You, O Lord, I will pray. In the morning You shall hear my voice: in the early morning I shall stand before You, and You will look upon me. For You are not a God who desires iniquity; nor shall he who works evil dwell in You; nor shall the transgressors abide before Your eyes: You have hated, O Lord, all who work iniquity. You will destroy all who speak falsehood. A man of blood and deceit the Lord abhors. But as for me, according to the multitude of Your mercy I shall enter Your house: I shall worship before Your holy temple in Your fear. Guide me, O Lord, in Your righteousness; for the sake of my enemies, make my way straight before You. For in their mouth there is no truth; their heart is vain; their throat is an open tomb; with their tongues they have done deceit. Judge them, O God; let them fall down in all their counsels: wipe them out according to the abundance of their ungodliness; for they have provoked You, O Lord. But let all who hope in You be glad: they shall rejoice for ever, and You shall dwell in them; and all who love Your name shall be proud in You. For You, O Lord, have blessed the righteous: as a shield of favor You have crowned us. ALLELUIA.

(6)   PSALM 6

O Lord, do not rebuke me in Your anger, nor chasten me in Your wrath. Have mercy on me, O Lord; for I am weak: heal me, O Lord, for my bones are troubled, and my soul is grievously troubled. But You, O Lord, how long? Return, deliver my soul: revive me for the sake of Your mercy. For in death there is no one who is remembering You: and in Hades who is able to confess to You? I became wearied in my groaning; I shall wash my bed every night; I shall wet my couch with my tears. My eye is troubled because of anger; I have grown old because of all my enemies.

Depart away from me, all who do iniquity; for the Lord has heard the voice of my weeping. The Lord has heard my petition; the Lord has accepted my prayer. All my enemies shall be put to shame and greatly troubled: they shall be turned back and put to shame speedily. ALLELUIA.

(7)   **PSALM 8**

O Lord, our Lord, how wonderful Your name became in all the earth! For the greatness of Your splendor has been exalted above the heavens. Out of the mouth of babes and sucklings You have prepared praise, because of Your enemies, that You might put down an enemy and avenger.

For I will regard the heavens, the work of Your fingers; the moon and stars You have established. What is man, that You have been mindful of him? Or the son of man, that You have visited him? You made him a little less than angels, You have crowned him with glory and honor; and You have set him upon the works of Your hands: You have put everything under his feet: all the sheep and oxen, and the beasts of the field, and the birds of the sky, and the fish of the sea that pass through the paths of the seas. O Lord our Lord, how wonderful Your name became in all the earth! ALLELUIA.

(8)   **PSALM 11**

Save me O Lord, for the godly one has ceased; and the truths have diminished from the children of men. Every one has spoken vanities to his friend. Deceiving lips are in their hearts, and thus they have spoken with their hearts. The Lord shall wipe out every deceiving lip, and every tongue that speaks great words; those who have said, "We will magnify our tongues; our lips are our own: who is lord over us?"

"Because of the misery of the poor and the sighing of the oppressed, now I will rise," says the Lord, "I will set them in salvation, and I will be revealed in it." The words of the Lord are pure words; as silver tried in the fire, proved in the earth, purified seven times. You, O Lord, shall keep us, and shall preserve us from this generation, and forever.   The ungodly walk around: according to Your greatness You have prolonged the lives of the children of men. ALLELUIA.

(9)　　　PSALM 12

How long, O Lord, do You forget me, for ever?
How long do You turn Your face away from
me? How long do I put these counsels in my
soul, and these sorrows in my heart for the
whole day? How long does my enemy exalt over
me? Look, hearken to me, O Lord my God:
enlighten my eyes, lest I sleep in death; lest my
enemy say, "I have prevailed against him": those
who distress me will rejoice if ever I stumble.
But I have hoped in Your mercy; my heart will
rejoice in Your salvation. I will praise the Lord
Who has done good to me, and I will sing to the
name of the Lord Most High. ALLELUIA.

(10)　　　PSALM 14

O Lord, who shall abide in Your dwelling place?
And who can rest upon Your holy mountain? It is
he who walks blamelessly, doing righteousness,
speaking truth in his heart, he who has not spoken
deceitfully with his tongue, neither has done evil
to his friend, nor taking up a reproach against his
neighbors. The evil worker is disdained before
him, but he glorifies those who fear the Lord. He
gives oath to his friend and does not turn away
from him. He has not given his money on usury,
and has not received bribes against the godly. He

who does these things shall not stumble forever.
ALLELUIA.

(11) **PSALM 15**

Keep me, O Lord; for I have hoped in You. I said to the Lord, "You are my Lord, and You have no need of my goodness." He has manifested His wonders to His saints who are in His earth, and He has wrought all His desires in them. Their ailments have been multiplied who hastened after another God. I will not assemble their meetings of blood, nor make mention of their names with my lips. The Lord is the portion of my inheritance and my cup. You are He who brings my inheritance back to me. The measuring lines have fallen to me among the best, and my inheritance is confirmed for me.

I will bless the Lord who has given me understanding; my reins too have instructed me even till the night. I foresaw the Lord always before me; He is on my right hand, that I should not be moved. Therefore my heart rejoiced and my tongue exulted; moreover also my flesh shall live in hope: because You shall not leave my soul in Hades, neither shall You suffer Your holy One to see corruption. You have made known to me the ways of life; You will fill me with joy with Your face: delight is in Your right hand forever. ALLELUIA.

(12)   PSALM 18

The heavens declare the glory of God; and the firmament proclaims the work of His hands. Day to day utters speech, and night to night proclaims knowledge. There are no speeches or words, in which their voice is not heard. Their sound has gone out upon all the earth, and their words have reached to the ends of the world. In the sun He has set His dwelling; and it comes forth as a bridegroom out of his chamber: it shall exult as a giant running his course. Its going forth is from the extremity of heaven, and its goal is to the other end of heaven: and nothing will be hidden from its heat.

The law of the Lord is pure, converting souls: the testimony of the Lord is faithful, instructing the babes. The ordinances of the Lord are straight, rejoicing the heart: the commandment of the Lord is a light, enlightening the eyes from afar. The fear of the Lord is pure, enduring forever and ever: the judgments of the Lord are true, and justified altogether. The desires of His heart are chosen more than gold and precious stone, and sweeter than honey and the honey-comb. For Your servant keeps them: and in keeping them there is great reward. Who can understand transgressions? From my secret sins cleanse me, O Lord, and from the attack of strangers spare Your servant: if they do not have dominion over me, then I shall be blameless, and I shall be cleansed from great sin. All the sayings of my mouth, and the meditation of my heart, shall be pleasing continually before You. O Lord; You are my helper, and my Savior. ALLELUIA.

(13)　　　**PSALM 24**

To You, O Lord, I have lifted up my soul. O my God, I have trusted in You: let me not be ashamed forever, nor let my enemies mock me. For all who wait for You shall not be ashamed: let them be ashamed who wrought iniquity in vain. Show me Your ways, O Lord; and teach me Your paths. Lead me to Your truth, and teach me: for You are God my Savior: and for You I have waited the whole day. Remember, O Lord, Your compassions and Your mercies, for they exist from everlasting. The sins of my youth and those of my ignorance do not remember; and according to Your mercy remember me, for the sake of Your goodness, O Lord.

For good and upright is the Lord: therefore He shall set a law for those who sin in the way. He shall guide the meek in judgment. He shall teach the meek His ways. All the ways of the Lord are mercy and truth to those who keep His covenant and His testimonies. For the sake of Your name, O Lord, You shall forgive my sin; for it is great. Who is the man that fears the Lord? He shall set a law for him in the way which pleases Him. His soul shall dwell in good things; and his seed shall inherit the earth. The Lord is the strength of those who fear Him; and the name of the Lord is for those who revere Him, and His covenant He will manifest to them. My eyes are ever looking towards the Lord; for He will draw my feet out of the snare. Look upon me, and have mercy on me; for I am an only child and poor. The afflictions of my heart have been multiplied; bring me out of my troubles. Behold my lowliness and my toil; and forgive all my sins. Look upon my enemies; for they have multiplied; and they have hated me with an unjust hatred. Keep my soul, and deliver me: Let me not be put to shame; for I have hoped in You. The harmless and upright joined themselves to me: for I waited for You, O Lord. Deliver Israel, O God, out of all his afflictions. ALLELUIA.

(14)   **PSALM 26**

The Lord is my light and my salvation; whom will I fear? The Lord is the defender of my life; of whom will I be afraid? When the wicked drew near against me to eat up my flesh, those who distress me and my enemies, they fainted and fell. Though an army should fight me, my heart shall not be afraid: though war should rise up against me, in this I am confident. One thing I have asked of the Lord, this also I will seek, that I should dwell in the house of the Lord all the days of my life, that I should behold the fair beauty of the Lord, and visit His holy temple. For in the day of my afflictions He hid me in His tabernacle: He sheltered me in the secret of His tabernacle; He set me up on a rock. And now, behold, He has lifted up my head over my enemies: I went round and offered in His tabernacle a sacrifice of joy; I shall sing, and sing psalms to the Lord. Hear, O Lord, my voice which I have uttered aloud: have mercy on me, and hearken to me. For You are He to whom my heart said, "I have sought Your face: Your face, O Lord, I will seek." Do not turn away Your face from me, do not reject Your servant in anger: be a helper to me, and do not forsake me; and do not overlook me, O God my Savior. For my father and my mother have forsaken me, but the Lord has accepted me unto Himself. Set a law for me, O Lord, in Your ways, and guide me in a right path, because of my enemies. Do not deliver me over to the souls of those who afflict me; for unjust witnesses have risen up against me, and injustice has lied to itself. I believe that I shall see the goodness of the Lord in the land of the living. Wait for the Lord: be of good cheer and let your heart be strengthened: and wait for the Lord. ALLELUIA.

(15)   PSALM 62

O God, my God, I will rise up early unto You; for my soul has thirsted for You: to make my flesh blossom for You, in a barren land and a trackless and dry place. So I have appeared before You in the Holy, to see Your power and Your glory. For Your mercy is chosen more than life: my lips shall praise You. So I will bless You during my life: I will lift up my hands in Your name. My soul shall be filled as with marrow and fatness; and lips of joy shall praise Your name. I have remembered You on my bed: in the time of early morning I have usually meditated on You. For You have become unto me a helper, and under the shadow of Your wings I shall rejoice. My soul has kept very close behind You: Your right hand has upheld me. But they vainly sought after my soul; they shall go into the lowest parts of the earth. They shall be delivered up to the hand of the sword; they shall be portions for foxes. But the king shall rejoice in God; everyone who swears by him shall be proud; for the mouths of those who speak unjust things shall be shut. ALLELUIA.

(16) **PSALM 66**

God shall pity us, and bless us; and reveal His face upon us and have mercy on us. That Your way may be known on the earth, Your salvation among all nations. Let the peoples, O God, give praise to You; let all the peoples give praise to You. Let the nations rejoice and exult, for You will judge peoples in equity, and guide nations on the earth. Let the peoples, O God, give praise to You; let all the peoples give praise to You. The earth has yielded its fruit. God, our God, shall bless us; and all the ends of the earth shall fear Him. ALLELUIA.

(17) **PSALM 69**

O God, be mindful to my help; make haste, O Lord, to help me. Let them be ashamed and be scorned, those who seek my soul: let them be turned backward and put to shame, those who wish to do evil unto me. Let those who say to me, "Aha, aha," be turned back in shame immediately. Let all who seek You exult and be glad in You: and let those who love Your salvation say continually, "Let the Lord be magnified." But I am poor and weak; O God, help me: You are my Helper and Savior, O Lord, do not delay. ALLELUIA.

(18)   PSALM 112

Praise the Lord, O the servants, praise the name of the Lord. Let the name of the Lord be blessed from now and forever. From the risings of the sun to its settings, praise the name of the Lord. The Lord is high above all the nations; upon the heavens is His glory. Who is like the Lord our God? Who dwells in the high places, and looks upon the low things in heaven and on the earth: who lifts up a poor person from the earth, and raises up a needy person from the ash heap; to seat him with the princes, even with the princes of his people: who makes a barren woman in a house, rejoicing as a mother of children. ALLELUIA.

(19)   PSALM 142

O Lord, hear my prayer: give ear to my supplication in Your truth; hearken to me in

Your justice. And do not enter into judgment with Your servant, for in Your sight no one living shall be justified. For the enemy has persecuted my soul; he has humbled my life down to the ground; he has made me to sit in darkness, as those who have been long dead. Therefore, my spirit grieves in me; my heart is troubled within me. I remembered the days of old; and I meditated on all Your doings: I meditated on the works of Your hands. I spread forth my hands unto You; my soul is toward You as a dry land.

Hear me quickly, O Lord, for my spirit has failed; do not turn away Your face from me, or I will be like those who go down to the pit. Let me hear Your mercy in the morning, for in You do I hope; make known to me, O Lord, the way in which I should walk, for I have lifted up my soul to You. Deliver me from my enemies, O Lord; for I have fled to You. Teach me to do Your will, for You are my God; Let Your Holy Spirit guide me in the straight way. You shall revive me, O Lord, for Your name's sake; in Your righteousness You shall bring my soul out of affliction. And in Your mercy You will wipe out my enemies, and destroy all who afflict my soul; for I am Your servant. ALLELUIA.

THE HOLY GOSPEL ACCORDING TO SAINT JOHN (1:1-17)

In the beginning was the Word, and the Word was with God, and the Word was God. He was in the beginning with God. All things were made by Him; and without Him was not anything made that was made. In Him was life; and the life was the light of men. And the light shines in darkness; and the darkness did not comprehend it. There was a man sent from God, whose name was John. This man came for a witness, to bear witness of the Light, that all men through him might believe. He was not the Light, but was sent to bear witness to the Light. That was the true Light that gives light to every man coming into the world. He was in the world, and the world was made by Him, and the world did not know Him. He came unto His own, and His own did not receive Him. But as many as received Him, to them He gave power to become children of God, to those who believe in His name: who were born, not of blood, nor of the will of the flesh, nor of the will of man, but of God. And the Word became flesh, and dwelt in us, and we beheld His glory, the glory as of the Only-Begotten of His Father, full of grace and truth.

John bore witness of Him, and cried out, saying, "This was He of whom I said, `He who comes after me is preferred before me: for He was before me.' " And of His fullness we have all received, and grace for grace. For the law was given by Moses, but grace and truth came through Jesus Christ. Glory be to God forever. Amen.

(Gospel Response: We worship You O Christ with Your Good Father and the Holy Spirit, for You have come and saved us.)

LITANIES

(1) O the true Light Who gives light to every man coming into the world, You came into the world through Your love for mankind, and all creation rejoiced in Your coming. You saved our father, Adam, from the seduction, and delivered our mother, Eve, from the pangs of death, and gave us the spirit of sonship. Let us, therefore, praise You and bless You saying:

Doxa Patri ke Eioa ke Agio Pnevmati (Glory to the Father, and the Son, and the Holy Spirit.)

(2) As the daylight shines upon us, O Christ Our God, the true Light, let the luminous senses and the bright thoughts shine within us, and do not let the darkness of passions hover over us, that mindfully we may praise You with David saying, "My eyes have awaken before the morning watch, that I might meditate on Your sayings." Hear our voices according to your great mercy, and deliver us, O Lord our God, through Your compassion.

Ke nin ke a e ke estos e onas ton e onon amin.
(Now and forever and unto the ages of all ages, Amen.)

(3) You are the honored Mother of the Light; from the risings of the sun to its settings praises are offered to you, O *Theotokos,* the second heaven, as you are the bright and unchanging flower, and the ever virgin mother; for the Father chose you, and the Holy Spirit overshadowed you, and the Son condescended and took flesh from you. Wherefore, ask Him to give salvation to the world which He created, and to deliver it from all tribulations. Let us praise Him a new praise, and bless Him, now and forever and unto the ages of all ages. Amen.

THE GLORIA

Let us praise with the angels, saying, "Glory to God in the highest, peace on earth, and good will toward men."We praise You. We bless You. We serve You. We worship You. We confess You. We glorify You. We give thanks to You for Your great glory, O Lord, King of heaven, God the Father, the Pantocrator *(Almighty)*; O Lord, the one and Only-Begotten Son, Jesus Christ, and the Holy Spirit.

O Lord God, Lamb of God, Son of the Father, Who takes away the sin of the world, have mercy on us. You, Who takes away the sin of the world, receive our prayers unto You. Who sits at the right hand of the Father, have mercy on us. You only are the Holy; You only are the Most High, Lord, Jesus Christ, with the Holy Spirit; glory to God the Father. Amen. Every day I will bless You, and praise Your holy name forever and unto the ages of ages. Amen. From the night season my soul awakes early unto You, O my God, for Your precepts are a light upon the earth. I was meditating on Your ways, for You have become a helper unto me. In the morning You shall hear my voice. Early I will stand before You, and You shall see me.

THE TRISAGION

Holy God, Holy Mighty, Holy Immortal, Who was born of the Virgin, have mercy on us.

Holy God, Holy Mighty, Holy Immortal, Who was crucified for us, have mercy on us.

Holy God, Holy Mighty, Holy Immortal, Who rose from the dead and ascended into the heavens, have mercy on us.

Glory to the Father, and to the Son, and to the Holy Spirit, now and forever and unto the ages of all ages. Amen.

O Holy Trinity, have mercy on us. O Holy Trinity, have mercy on us. O Holy Trinity, have mercy on us.

O Lord, forgive us our sins. O Lord, forgive us our iniquities. O Lord, forgive us our trespasses.

O Lord, visit the sick of Your people, heal them for the sake of Your holy name. Our fathers and brothers who have slept, O Lord, repose their souls.

O You Who are without sin, Lord have mercy on us. O You Who are without sin, Lord help us and receive our supplications. For Yours is the glory, the dominion, and triple holiness. Lord have mercy. Lord have mercy. Lord bless. Amen.

Make us worthy to pray thankfully:
Our Father Who art in heaven ...

HAIL TO SAINT MARY

Hail to you. We ask you, O saint, full of glory, the ever virgin, the Theotokos (*Mother of God*), the Mother of Christ, lift up our prayers unto your beloved Son, that He may forgive us our sins.

Hail to the Holy Virgin, who bore for us the true Light, Christ our God. Ask the Lord on our behalf, that He may have mercy on our souls, and forgive us our sins.

O Virgin Mary, the holy Theotokos (*Mother of God*),* the trusted advocate of the human race, intercede on our behalf before Christ, Whom you bore, that He may grant us the forgiveness of our sins.

Hail to you, O Virgin, the right and true queen. Hail to the pride of our race, you bore for us Emmanuel.

We ask you, remember us, our trusted advocate, before our Lord Jesus Christ, that He may forgive us our sins.

INTRODUCTION TO THE CREED

We exalt you, the Mother of the true Light. We glorify you, O Saint, the Theotokos, for you brought forth unto us the Savior of the whole world; He came and saved our souls.

Glory to You, our Master, our King, Christ, the pride of the apostles, the crown of the martyrs, the joy of the righteous, the firmness of the churches, the forgiveness of sins.

We proclaim the Holy Trinity in One Godhead. We worship Him. We glorify Him.

Lord have mercy. Lord have mercy. Lord bless. Amen.

THE ORTHODOX CREED

We believe in one God, God the Father, the Pantocrator (*Almighty),* Who created heaven and earth, and all things, seen and unseen.

We believe in one Lord Jesus Christ, the Only-Begotten Son of God, begotten of the Father before all ages; Light of Light, true God of true God, begotten not created, of one essence with the Father, by Whom all things were made; Who for us, men, and for our salvation, came down from heaven, and was incarnated of the Holy

Spirit and of the Virgin Mary, and became man. And He was crucified for us under Pontius Pilate, suffered and was buried. And on the third day He rose from the dead, according to the Scriptures, and ascended into the heavens; and sat at the right hand of His Father, and also He is coming again in His glory to judge the living and the dead, whose kingdom has no end.

Yes, we believe in the Holy Spirit, the Lord, the Life-Giver, Who proceeds from the Father, Who, with the Father and the Son, is worshipped and glorified, Who spoke in the prophets. And in one holy, *catholic (universal)* and apostolic church. We confess one baptism for the remission of sins.

We look for the resurrection of the dead, and the life of the coming age. Amen.

Then the worshipper prays:

Lord, hear us and have mercy on us and forgive us our sins. Amen.

Kyrie eleison (Lord have mercy)
is prayed 41 times

HOLY HOLY HOLY

Holy Holy Holy. Lord of hosts. Heaven and earth are full of Your glory and honor. Have mercy on us, O God the Father, the Pantocrator (*Almighty*) O Holy Trinity, have mercy on us. O Lord, God of hosts, be with us. For we have no helper in our hardships and tribulations but You. Absolve, forgive, and remit, O God, our transgressions; those which we have committed willingly and those we have committed unwillingly, those which we have committed knowingly and those which we have committed unknowingly, the hidden and manifest, O Lord forgive us, for the sake of Your Holy name which is called upon us. Let it be according to Your mercy, O Lord, and not according to our sins.

Make us worthy to pray thankfully: *Our Father..*

FIRST ABSOLUTION

O Lord, God of hosts, who exists before all ages and abides forever, who created the sun for daylight, and the night as rest for all men; we thank You, O King of ages, for You have let us pass through the night in peace, and brought us to the daybreak. Therefore, we ask You, O our Master, the King of all ages, to let Your face shine upon us, and the light of Your divine knowledge enlighten us. Grant us, O our Master, to be sons of light and sons of day, to pass this day in righteousness, chastity and good conduct, that we may complete all the rest of the days of our life without offence; through the grace, the compassion and the love of mankind of Your Only-Begotten Son Jesus Christ, and the gift of Your Holy Spirit, now and at all times and forever. Amen.

SECOND ABSOLUTION

O God Who causes the light to burst forth, Who lets His sun shine upon the righteous and the wicked, Who created the light which illuminates the whole world, enlighten our minds, our hearts and our understandings, O Master of all, and grant us to please You this present day. Guard us from every bad thing, from every sin, and from every adverse power; through Christ Jesus our Lord, with whom You are blessed, with the Holy Spirit, the Life-Giver and one essence with You, now and at all times and unto the ages of all ages. Amen.

CONCLUSION OF EVERY HOUR

Have mercy on us, O God, and have mercy on us, who, at all times and in every hour, in heaven and on earth, is worshipped and glorified, Christ our God, the good, the long suffering, the abundant in mercy, and the great in compassion, who loves the righteous and has mercy on the sinners of whom I am chief; who does not wish the death of the sinner but rather that he returns and lives, who calls all to salvation for the promise of the blessings to come. Lord receive from us our prayers in this hour and in every hour. Ease our life and guide us to fulfill Your commandments. Sanctify our spirits. Cleanse our bodies. Conduct our thoughts. Purify our intentions. Heal our diseases. Forgive our sins. Deliver us from every evil grief and distress of heart. Surround us by Your holy angels, that, by their camp, we may be guarded and guided, and attain the unity of faith, and the knowledge of Your imperceptible and infinite glory. For You are blessed forever. Amen.

The Third Hour

(At this hour, it was the Christ's trial by Pilate and the descent of the Holy Spirit upon the disciples.)

INTRODUCTION TO EVERY HOUR

In the name of the Father, and the Son, and the Holy Spirit, one God. Amen.
Kyrie eleison. Lord have mercy, Lord have mercy, Lord bless us. Amen.
Glory to the Father, and to the Son, and to the Holy Spirit, now and forever and unto the ages of all ages. Amen.
The prayer of the Third Hour of the blessed day, we offer to Christ our King and our God, beseeching Him to forgive us our sins.
From the Psalms of our father David the prophet and the king, may his blessings be upon us all. Amen.

(1)   **PSALM 19**

The Lord shall hear you in the day of your trouble, the name of the God of Jacob defend you. He shall send you help from His Holy, and uphold you out of Zion. He shall remember all your sacrifices, and enrich your burnt offerings. The Lord shall grant you according to your heart, and fulfill all your counsel. We will confess your salvation, and in the name of our God we shall grow: the Lord shall fulfill all your petitions. Now I know that the Lord has saved His anointed: He shall hear him from His holy heaven, the salvation of His right hand is in mighty deeds. These in chariots, and these in horses, but in the name of the Lord our God we will grow. They are overthrown and fallen, but we risen, and set upright. O Lord, save Your king: and hear us in the day we call upon You. ALLELUIA.

(2)   **PSALM 22**

The Lord is He who shepherds me; I shall need nothing. In a place of green pasture, there He has made me dwell: by the water of rest, He has tended me. He has restored my soul: He has guided me into the paths of righteousness, for His name's sake. Even if I walk in the midst of the shadow of death, I shall not fear evil things, for You are with me: Your rod and Your staff, these comfort me. You have prepared a table before me in the presence of those who afflict me: You have anointed my head with oil; and Your cup makes me drunk like power. Your mercy shall follow me all the days of my life: and my dwelling shall be in the house of the Lord unto length of days. ALLELUIA.

(3)   **PSALM 23**

The earth and its fullness are the Lord's; the world and all that dwell in it. He has founded it upon the seas, and prepared it upon the rivers. Who shall go up to the mountain of the Lord, and who shall stand in His holy place? He that is pure in his hands, and clean in his heart; who has not lifted up his soul in vanity, nor sworn deceitfully to his neighbor. He shall receive a blessing from the Lord, and mercy from God his Savior. This is the generation of those who seek the Lord, who seek the face of the God of Jacob. Lift up your gates, you princes, and be lifted up, you everlasting doors; and the king of glory shall come in. Who is this king of glory? The Lord who is strong and mighty, the Lord who is mighty in war. Lift up your gates, you princes;

and be lifted up, you everlasting doors; and the king of glory shall come in. Who is this king of glory? The Lord of hosts, He is this king of glory. ALLELUIA.

(4)   **PSALM 25**

Judge me, O Lord; for I have walked in my innocence: and trusted in the Lord, I shall not be weakened. Prove me, O Lord, and try me; purify my heart and my reins. For your mercy is before my eyes: and I am pleased with your truth. I have not sat with the vain council, nor shall I enter in with the transgressors. I have hated the assembly of evil doers; and shall not sit with ungodly men. I will wash my hands in purity, and go around Your altar, O Lord, to hear the voice of Your praise, and to speak of all Your wonderful works. O Lord, I have loved the beauty of Your house, and the dwelling place of Your glory. Do not destroy my soul together with the ungodly, nor my life with bloody men: in whose hands are iniquity, and their right hand is filled with bribe. But I have walked in my innocence: save me, and have mercy upon me. My foot stood in uprightness: in the congregations I will praise You, O Lord. ALLELUIA.

(5) **PSALM 28**

Bring to the Lord, O sons of God, bring to the Lord young rams; bring to the Lord glory and honor. Bring to the Lord glory to His name; worship the Lord in His holy court.

The voice of the Lord is upon the waters: God of glory has thundered: the Lord is upon the many waters. The voice of the Lord is mighty; the voice of the Lord is in great beauty. The voice of the Lord breaks the cedar; the Lord will break the cedar of Lebanon. And He will beat them small like the calf of Lebanon; and the beloved one like a son of the unicorn.

The voice of the Lord cuts a flame of fire. The voice of the Lord shakes the wilderness; the Lord will shake the wilderness of Kadesh. The voice of the Lord strengthens the deer, and will uncover the forests: and in His holy temple every one speaks of glory.

The Lord dwells in the flood: and the Lord will sit as a king forever. The Lord will give strength to His people; the Lord will bless His people with peace. ALLELUIA.

(6)   PSALM 29

I will exalt You, O Lord; for You have accepted
me, and not caused my enemies to rejoice over
me. O Lord, my God, I cried to You, and You
have healed me. O Lord, You have brought up
my soul from Hades, You have delivered me
from the hands of those who will go down to the
pit.

Sing to the Lord, all you His saints, and confess
the remembrance of His holiness. For anger is in
His wrath, but life in His favor: weeping shall be
for the evening, but joy shall be in the morning.
I said in my prosperity, I shall never be moved.
O Lord, in Your will You gave strength to my
beauty: but You turned away Your face from
me, and I became troubled. To You, O Lord, I
shall cry; and to my God I shall make
supplication. What profit is there in my blood,
when I go down to destruction? Shall the dust
confess to You? or shall it declare Your truth?
The Lord heard, and had mercy upon me; the
Lord became to me a helper. You have turned
my mourning into joy for me: You have rent off
my sackcloth, and girded me with gladness; that
my glory may sing praise to You, and I shall not
be troubled at heart. O Lord, my God, I will
confess to You forever. ALLELUIA.

(7)   **PSALM 33**

I will bless the Lord at all times: His praise shall
be continually in my mouth. My soul shall boast
herself in the Lord: let the meek hear and
rejoice. Magnify the Lord with me, and let us
exalt His name together. I sought the Lord
diligently, and He heard me, and delivered me
from all my fear. Draw near to Him, and be
enlightened: and your faces shall not be
ashamed. This poor man cried, and the Lord
heard him, and delivered him out of all his
afflictions. The angel of the Lord will encamp
round about those who fear Him, and will
deliver them. Taste and see that the Lord is
sweet: blessed is the man who hopes in Him.
Fear the Lord, all you His saints: for there is no
want to those who fear Him. The rich have
become poor and they hungered: but those who
seek the Lord shall not want any good thing.

Come, you children, hear me: I will teach you
the fear of the Lord. Who is the man that desires
life, and is thinking to see good days? Keep your
tongue from evil, and your lips from speaking
guile. Turn away from evil, and do good; seek
peace, and pursue it. For the eyes of the Lord are
over the righteous, and His ears are bent to their
prayer: but the face of the Lord is against those

who do evil, to wipe out their memorial from upon the earth. The righteous cried, and the Lord heard them, and delivered them out of all their afflictions. The Lord is near to those who are contrite in their heart; and will save the lowly in spirit. Many are the afflictions of the righteous: but out of them all the Lord will deliver them. The Lord will keep all their bones: not one of them shall be broken. The death of the sinners is evil: and those who hate righteousness will grieve. The Lord will save the souls of His servants: and none of those who hope in Him shall grieve. ALLELUIA.

(8)   **PSALM 40**

Blessed is he who thinks of the poor and needy: the Lord shall deliver him in an evil day. The Lord shall preserve him and keep him alive, and make him blessed on the earth, and not deliver him into the hands of his enemies. The Lord shall help him upon the bed of his pain; You have made all his bed in his sickness. I said, O Lord, have mercy on me; heal my soul; for I have sinned against You. My enemies have spoken evil against me, saying, "When shall he die, and his name perish?" And if he came to see me, he spoke in vanity; and his heart gathered unto him iniquity; he went forth and spoke in like manner. All my enemies whispered against me; against me they devised evil. They denounced a wicked word against me, saying, "Now that he lies, shall he not rise up again?" For even the man of my peace, he whom I trusted, who ate my bread, lifted up his heel against me. But you, O Lord, have mercy upon me, and raise me up, and I shall compensate them. In this I knew that You were delighted in me, because my enemy shall not rejoice over me. But because of my innocence You accepted me, and have established me before You forever. Blessed be the Lord God of Israel, from everlasting and to everlasting. So be it, so be it. ALLELUIA.

(9)   PSALM 42

Judge me, O Lord, and avenge my case, against an impure nation: You shall deliver me from the unjust and crafty man. For You are my God and my strength: why have You cast me off? And why do I walk gloomingly, while the enemy oppresses me? Send forth Your light and Your truth: they have led me, and brought me to Your holy mountain, and to Your dwelling. And I will go into the altar of God, before the face of God

who gladdens my youth: I will give praise to You
with the harp, O God, my God. Why are you sad,
O my soul? and why do you trouble me? Hope in
God; for I will give thanks to Him. The salvation
of my face is my God. ALLELUIA.

(10)   PSALM 44
My heart has poured forth a good word: I will
declare my works to the King: my tongue is a
writer's pen, sharpened for writing. You are comely
in beauty more than the sons of men: grace has
been shed forth from Your lips: therefore God has
blessed You forever. Gird Your sword upon Your
thigh, O Mighty One, in Your comeliness, and in
Your beauty; draw it, prosper, and reign, because
of truth and meekness and righteousness; and Your
right hand shall guide You wonderfully. Your
arrows are sharp, O Mighty One, in the heart of the
King's enemies; the nations shall fall under You.
Your throne, O God, is for ever and ever: the
scepter of Your kingdom is a scepter of
uprightness. You have loved righteousness, and
hated iniquity: therefore, God, Your God, has
anointed You with the oil of gladness more than
Your fellows. Myrrh and stacte and cassia are from
Your garments, and out of the ivory palaces, with
which they have gladdened You; Kings' daughters

for Your honor. The queen stood by on Your right hand, clothed in a vestment wrought with gold work, and adorned in divers manners. Hear, O my daughter, and see, and incline your ear; forget your people, and your father's house. Because the King has desired your beauty; for indeed He is your Lord, and you shall worship Him. The daughters of Tyre shall worship Him with gifts; the rich of the people of the land shall supplicate His favor. All the glory of the daughter of the King is within, robed in golden fringed garments, adorned in various manners. Virgins shall be brought to the King after her: all her fellows shall be brought to Him. They shall be brought with gladness and exultation: they shall be brought into the King's temple. Instead of Your fathers, children shall be unto You: You shall make them princes over all the earth. They shall make mention of Your name from generation to generation: therefore the nations shall give praise to You, O God, forever, even forever and ever. ALLELUIA.

(11) **PSALM 45**

God is our refuge and our strength; He is our help in the afflictions that have come heavily upon us. Therefore we shall not fear when the earth is troubled, and the mountains are removed into the heart of the seas. The waters have roared and been troubled, the mountains have been troubled by His might. The streams of the river gladden the city of God: the Most High has sanctified His dwelling. God is in the midst of her; she shall not be moved: God shall help her face. The nations were troubled, the kingdoms tottered: He gave forth His voice, the earth shook. The Lord, God of hosts, is with us; the God of Jacob is our helper.

Come, you, and behold the works of the Lord, the wonders which He has set upon the earth. Putting an end to wars to the ends of the earth; He will crush their bows, and break their weapons, and burn their bucklers in the fire. Be still, and know that I am God: I will be exalted among the nations, I will be exalted upon the earth. The Lord God of hosts is with us; the God of Jacob is our helper. ALLELUIA.

(12)   PSALM 46

Clap your hands, all you nations; shout to God with a voice of exultation. For the Lord is most high and fearful; He is a great king over all the earth. He has subdued peoples under us, and nations under our feet. He has chosen us for His inheritance, the beauty of Jacob He loved.

God has ascended with a shout, and the Lord with a sound of a trumpet. Sing praises to our God, sing praises: sing praises to our King, sing praises; for God is king of all the earth. Sing praises with understanding, for the Lord reigned over all the nations: God sits upon His holy throne. Rulers of the people have assembled with God of Abraham: for God's mighty ones have been greatly exalted upon the earth. ALLELUIA.

THE HOLY GOSPEL ACCORDING TO ST. JOHN (CH. 14:26-31 & CH. 15:1-4)

When the Comforter, the Holy Spirit, Whom the Father will send in My name, has come, He shall teach you all things, and bring to your remembrance all things that I have said unto you. My peace I leave with you, My peace I give unto you: not as the world gives do I give unto you. Let not your heart be troubled, neither let it be afraid. You have heard how I said unto you, "I go away, and come again unto you." If you loved Me, you would rejoice, because I said, "I go unto the Father": for My Father is greater than I.

And now I have told you before it comes to pass, that, when it comes to pass, you might believe. I will not talk much with you: for the prince of this world comes, and has nothing in Me. But that the world may know that I love the Father; and as the Father gave Me commandment, so I do: arise, let us go from here. I am the true vine, and My Father is the vinedresser. Every branch in Me that does not bear fruit He takes away: and every branch that bears fruit He prunes, that it may bring forth more fruit. Now you are clean through the word which I have spoken unto you. Abide in Me, and I in you. Glory to God forever. Amen.

LITANIES

(1) Your Holy Spirit, O Lord Whom You sent forth upon Your holy disciples and honored apostles in the third hour, do not take away from us, O Good One, but renew Him within us. Create in me a clean heart, O God, and renew a right spirit within me. Do not cast me away from Your presence and do not take Your Holy Spirit away from me. *(Doxa Patri ke Eioa ke Agio Pnevmati)*

(2) O Lord who sent down Your Holy Spirit upon Your holy disciples and Your honored apostles in the third hour, do not take Him away from us, O Good One, but we ask You to renew Him within us, O Lord Jesus Christ, Son of God, the Word; a right and life-giving spirit, a spirit of prophecy and chastity, a spirit of holiness, righteousness and authority, O the Almighty One, for You are the light of our souls. O You Who gives light to every man that comes into the world, have mercy on us. (*Ke nin ke a e ke estos e onas ton e onon amin.*)

(3) O Theotokos (*Mother of God*), you are the true vine who bore the Cluster of Life, we ask you, O full of grace, with the apostles, for the salvation of our souls. Blessed is the Lord our God. Blessed is the Lord day by day. He prepares our way, for He is God of our salvation. *(Ke nin ke a e ke estos e onas ton e onon amin.)*

(4) O Heavenly King, the Comforter, the Spirit of truth, who is present in all places and fills all, the treasury of good things and the Life-Giver, graciously come, and dwell in us and purify us from all defilement, O Good One, and save our souls. *(Doxa Patri ke Eioa ke Agio Pnevmati)*

(5) Just as You were with Your disciples, O Savior, and gave them peace, graciously come also and be with us, and grant us Your peace, and save us, and deliver our souls. *(Ke nin ke a e ke estos e onas ton e onon amin.)*

(6) Whenever we stand in Your holy sanctuary, we are considered standing in heaven. O Theotokos, you are the gate of heaven, open for us the gate of mercy.

Lord, hear us and have mercy on us and forgive us our sins. Amen.

> **Kyrie eleison, Lord have mercy (41 times)**
> **HOLY HOLY HOLY   page 64**
> **Our Father who art in Heaven...**

ABSOLUTION

O God of all compassion, and Lord of all comfort, who comforted us at all times with the comfort of Your Holy Spirit, we thank You for You raised us for prayer in this holy hour, in which You abundantly poured the grace of Your Holy Spirit upon Your holy disciples and honorable and blessed apostles, like tongues of fire.

We ask and entreat You, O lover of mankind, to accept our prayers, and forgive our sins, and send forth upon us the grace of Your Holy Spirit, and purify us from all defilement of body and spirit.

Change us into a spiritual manner of life, that we may walk in the Spirit and not fulfill the lusts of the flesh. And make us worthy to serve You with purity and righteousness all the days of our life. For unto You is due glory, honor, and dominion, with Your good Father and the Holy Spirit, now and forever and unto the ages of all ages. Amen.

THE CONCLUSION OF EVERY HOUR
page 68

The Sixth Hour

(At this hour, our Lord Jesus Christ was crucified.)

In the name of the Father, and the Son, and the Holy Spirit, one God. Amen.

Kyrie eleison. Lord have mercy, Lord have mercy, Lord bless us. Amen.

Glory to the Father, and to the Son, and to the Holy Spirit, now and forever and unto the ages of all ages. Amen.

The prayer of the Sixth Hour of the blessed day, we offer to Christ our King and our God, beseeching Him to forgive us our sins.

From the Psalms of our father David the prophet and the king, may his blessings be upon us all. Amen.

(1) PSALM 53

Save me, O God, by Your name, and judge me by Your power. O God, hear my prayer; hearken to the words of my mouth. For strangers have risen up against me, and mighty men have sought my soul: they have not set God before them. For behold, God helped me; and the Lord is the protector of my soul. He shall return the evil things to my enemies; utterly wipe them out by Your truth. I will willingly sacrifice to You: I will confess Your name, O Lord; for it is good. For You have delivered me out of every affliction, and my eye has looked down upon my enemies. ALLELUIA.

(2) PSALM 56

Have mercy upon me, O God, have mercy upon me: for my soul has trusted in You: and in the shadow of Your wings I will hope, until the iniquity passes away. I will cry to God Most High; God who has benefited me. He sent from heaven and saved me; He gave over to reproach those who trampled on me: God has sent forth His mercy and His truth; and He has delivered my soul from the midst of young lions: I laid down to sleep, while troubled. As for the sons of men, their teeth are weapons and arrows, and their tongue a sharp sword. Be You exalted, O God, above the heavens; and Your glory above all the earth. They have prepared snares for my feet, and have bowed down my soul: they have dug a pit before me, and fallen into it. My heart, O God, is ready, my heart is ready: I will sing, and chant in my glory. Arise, my glory; arise, psaltery and harp: I will rise early. O Lord, I will confess You among the peoples: I will sing to You among the nations. For Your mercy has been magnified up to the heavens, and Your truth up to the clouds. Be You exalted, O God, above the heavens; and Your glory above all the earth. ALLELUIA.

(3) PSALM 60

Hear, O God, my petition; attend to my prayer. From the ends of the earth I have cried to You, when my heart was in trouble: You elevated me up on a rock, You guided me: You became a hope, a tower of power from the face of an enemy. I shall dwell in Your dwelling place forever; I shall be sheltered under the shadow of Your wings. For You, O God, have heard my prayers; You have given an inheritance to those who fear Your name. Days upon days of the king, You shall lengthen his years to all generations. He shall endure forever before God. As for His mercy and truth, who will be able to seek them out? So I will sing to Your name forever and ever, that I may perform my vows day by day. ALLELUIA.

(4)   **PSALM 62**

O God, my God, I will rise up early unto You; for my soul has thirsted for You: to make my flesh blossom for You, in a barren land and a trackless and dry place. So I have appeared before You in the Holy, to see Your power and Your glory. For Your mercy is chosen more than life: my lips shall praise You. So I will bless You during my life: I will lift up my hands in Your name. My soul shall be filled as with marrow and fatness; and lips of joy shall praise Your name. I have remembered You on my bed: in the time of early morning I have usually meditated on You. For You have become unto me a helper, and under the shadow of Your wings I shall rejoice.

My soul has kept very close behind You: Your right hand has upheld me. But they vainly sought after my soul; they shall go into the lowest parts of the earth. They shall be delivered up to the hand of the sword; they shall be portions for foxes. But the king shall rejoice in God; everyone who swears by him shall be proud; for the mouths of those who speak unjust things shall be shut. ALLELUIA.

(5)   PSALM 66

God shall pity us, and bless us; and reveal His face upon us and have mercy on us. That Your way may be known on the earth, Your salvation among all nations. Let the peoples, O God, give praise to You; let all the peoples give praise to You. Let the nations rejoice and exult, for You will judge peoples in equity, and guide nations on the earth. Let the peoples, O God, give praise to You; let all the peoples give praise to You. The earth has yielded its fruit. God, our God, shall bless us; and all the ends of the earth shall fear Him. ALLELUIA.

(6)   PSALM 69

O God, be mindful of my help; make haste, O Lord, to help me. Let them be ashamed and be scorned, those who seek my soul: let them be turned backward and put to shame, those who wish to do evil unto me. Let those who say to me, "Aha, aha," be turned back in shame immediately. Let all who seek You exult and be glad in You: and let those who love Your salvation say continually, "Let the Lord be magnified." But I am poor and weak; O God, help me: You are my Helper and Savior, O Lord, do not delay. ALLELUIA.

(7)   **PSALM 83**

How beloved are Your dwellings, O Lord, God of hosts! My soul longs, and faints for the courts of the Lord: my heart and my flesh have exulted in the living God. For, the sparrow has found for himself a home, and the turtledove for herself a nest, where she may lay her young; Your altars, O Lord, God of hosts, my King, and my God. Blessed are all who dwell in Your house: they will praise You forever and ever. Blessed is the man whose help is from You, O Lord; he sets paths upward in his heart in the valley of weeping, in the place which he has appointed, for there the Law-Giver will grant blessings. They shall go from strength to strength: the God of gods shall be revealed in Zion. O Lord, God of hosts, hear my prayer: hearken, O God of Jacob. Behold, O God our defender, and look upon the face of Your anointed. For one day in Your courts is better than thousands.

I chose to throw myself down in the house of God, more than to dwell in the tents of the sinners. For the Lord God loves mercy and truth; He shall give grace and glory: the Lord shall not withhold good things from those who walk in innocence. O Lord God of hosts, blessed is the man who hopes in You. ALLELUIA.

(8) PSALM 84

O Lord, You have taken pleasure in Your land: You have turned back the captivity of Jacob. You have forgiven the transgressions of Your people: You have covered all their sins. You have dissolved all Your wrath: You have turned from the wrath of Your anger. Turn us, O God of our salvation, and turn Your anger away from us. Would You be angry with us forever? Or will You extend Your wrath from generation to generation? O God, You shall turn back and revive us; and Your people shall rejoice in You. Show us Your mercy, O Lord, and grant us Your salvation. I will hear what the Lord God will speak in me: for He shall speak peace to His people, and to His saints, and to those who turned back to Him with all their heart. Surely His salvation is near to all who fear Him; to make glory dwell in our land. Mercy and truth have met together: righteousness and peace have greeted each other. Truth has sprung out of the earth; and righteousness has looked down from heaven. For the Lord shall give goodness; and our land shall yield its fruit. Righteousness shall go first before Him; and shall set His steps in the way. ALLELUIA.

(9) **PSALM 85**

Incline Your ear, O Lord, and hear me; for I am poor and weak. Preserve my soul, for I am pure; save Your servant, O my God, who hopes in You. Have mercy on me, O Lord: for to You I will cry the whole day. Rejoice the soul of Your servant: for to You, O Lord, I have lifted up my soul. For You, O Lord, are righteous, and gentle; and plenteous is Your mercy to all who call upon You. Give ear to my prayer, O Lord; and attend to the voice of my supplication. In the day of my trouble I cried to You: for You heard me. There is none like You, O Lord, among the gods; and there is none that is able to do Your works. All nations whom You have made shall come, and shall worship before You, O Lord; and shall glorify Your name. For You are great, and wondrous: You alone are the great God. Guide me, O Lord, in Your way, and I shall walk in Your truth: let my heart rejoice, that I may fear Your name. I will confess You, O Lord my God, with all my heart; and I will glorify Your name forever. For Your mercy is great toward me; and You have delivered my soul from the lowest Hades. O God, transgressors have risen up against me, and an assembly of violent men have sought my soul; and have not, at first, set You before them. But You, O Lord God, are compassionate and merciful, long-suffering, and abundant in mercy and true. Look down upon me, and have mercy on me: give strength to Your servant, and save the son of Your handmaid. Establish with me a sign for good; and let those who hate me see and be ashamed; because You, O Lord, have helped me, and comforted me. ALLELUIA.

(10)   PSALM 86

His foundations are in the holy mountains. The Lord loves the gates of Zion, more than all the dwellings of Jacob. Glorious things have been spoken of You, O city of God. I shall make mention of Raab and Babylon, those who know me: behold the foreigners, and Tyre, and the people of Ethiopia: these were there. "My mother Zion," a man will say; and a man was living in her: and the Most High Himself has founded her forever. The Lord shall tell it in the writings of peoples and princes, these who were in her. The dwelling of all who rejoice is within you. ALLELUIA.

(11)   **PSALM 90**

He who dwells in the help of the Most High, shall rest under the shelter of the God of heaven. He shall say to the Lord, "You are my defender and my refuge: my God; I will hope in Him." For He shall deliver you from the snare of the hunter, and from troublesome matter. He shall overshadow you in the midst of His shoulders, and you shall hope under His wings: His truth shall encompass you as a shield. You shall not be afraid of the terror of the night; nor of an arrow flying in the day; nor of a matter walking in darkness; nor of calamity and demon of noon-day. A thousand shall fall at your left hand, and ten thousand at your right hand; but they shall not be able to come near you. Only with your eyes shall you observe, and see the reward of sinners. For You, O Lord, are my hope. You have made the Most High your refuge. No evil things shall come upon you, and no plague shall draw near to your dwelling. For

He shall give his angels charge concerning you, to keep you in all your ways. They shall bear you up on their hands, lest you stumble Your foot against a stone. You shall tread on the serpent and basilisk: and You shall trample on the lion and dragon. For he has hoped in Me, and I shall deliver him: I shall protect him, because he has known My name. He shall beseech Me, and I shall hear him: I am with him in affliction; and I shall deliver him, and glorify him. I shall satisfy him with length of days, and show him My salvation. ALLELUIA.

(12)   PSALM 92

The Lord has reigned; He has clothed Himself with beauty: the Lord has clothed and girded Himself with strength; for He has established the world, which shall not be moved. Your throne is prepared from the beginning: You are from everlasting. The rivers have risen, O Lord; the rivers have elevated their voices: the rivers shall elevate their voices, from the voices of many waters. The billows of the waves of the sea are wonderful: the Lord is wonderful in the highest. His testimonies are very faithful: holiness is worthy of Your house, O Lord, unto length of days. ALLELUIA.

THE HOLY GOSPEL ACCORDING TO ST. MATTHEW (CH. 5 : 1-16)

And seeing the multitudes, He went up on a mountain, and when He was seated, His disciples came to Him. And He opened His mouth, and taught them, saying:

"Blessed are the poor in spirit, for theirs is the kingdom of heaven. Blessed are those who mourn, for they shall be comforted. Blessed are the meek, for they shall inherit the earth. Blessed are those who hunger and thirst for righteousness, for they shall be filled. Blessed are the merciful, for they shall obtain mercy. Blessed are the pure in heart, for they shall see God. Blessed are the peacemakers, for they shall be called sons of God. Blessed are those who are persecuted for righteousness' sake, for theirs is the kingdom of heaven.

"Blessed are you, when they revile you, and persecute you, and say all kinds of evil against you falsely for My sake. Rejoice and be exceedingly glad, for great is your reward in heaven, for so they persecuted the prophets who were before you.

"You are the salt of the earth; but if the salt loses its flavor, how shall it be seasoned? It is then good for nothing but to be thrown out and trampled underfoot by men. "You are the light of the world. A city that is set on a hill cannot be hidden; nor do they light a lamp and put it under a basket, but on a lamp stand, and it gives light to all who are in the house. "Let your light so shine before men, that they may see your good works, and glorify your Father Who is in heaven."

Glory to God forever. Amen.

LITANIES

(1) O You, Who on the sixth day and in the sixth hour was nailed to the cross, for the sin which our father Adam dared to commit in Paradise, tear the handwriting of our sins, O Christ our God, and save us. I cried to the Lord and He heard me. God hear my prayer, and do not refuse my petition. Be attentive to me and hear me in the evening, in the morning, and at midday. I say my words, and He hears my voice and delivers my soul in peace. *(Doxa Patri ..)*

(2) O Jesus Christ, our God, who was nailed to the cross in the sixth hour, and killed sin by the tree, and by Your death You made alive the dead man, whom You created with Your own hands, and had died in sin. Put to death our pains by Your healing and life-giving passions, and by the nails with which You were nailed. Rescue our minds from thoughtlessness of the earthly deeds and worldly lusts, to the remembrance of Your heavenly commandments, according to Your compassion. *(Ke nin ..)*

(3) Since we have no favor, nor excuse, nor justification because of our many sins, we, through you, implore to Him who was born of you, O Theotokos, the Virgin, for abundant and acceptable is your intercession with our Savior. O pure mother, do not exclude sinners from your intercession with Him whom you bore, for He is merciful and able to save us, because He suffered for us to deliver us. Let your compassion speedily reach us, for we are exceedingly humbled. Help us, O God, our Savior, for the glory of Your name. O Lord, deliver us and forgive us our sins for the sake of Your holy name. *(Ke nin ..)*

(4) You wrought salvation in the midst of all the earth, O Christ our God, as You stretched Your holy hands on the cross. Therefore, all nations cry out saying, "Glory to You O Lord". *(Doxa Patri..)*

(5) We worship Your incorruptible person, O Good One, asking for the forgiveness of our sins, O Christ our God. For, of Your will, You were pleased to be lifted up onto the cross, to deliver those whom You created from the bondage of the enemy. We cry out unto You and give thanks to You, for You have filled all with joy, O Savior, when You came to help the world. Lord, glory be to You. *(Ke nin..)*

(6) You are she who is full of grace. O Theotokos, the Virgin, we praise you, for, through the cross of your Son, Hades fell down and death was abolished. We were dead but we are raised and became worthy of eternal life, and gained the delight of the first Paradise. Therefore, we thankfully glorify the immortal Christ our God.

> **Kyrie eleison, Lord have mercy (41 times)**
> **HOLY HOLY HOLY   page 64**
> **Our Father who art in Heaven...**

ABSOLUTION

We thank You, our King, the Almighty, the Father of our Lord God and Savior Jesus Christ, and glorify You, for You have made the times of the passions of Your Only-Begotten Son, to be times of comfort and prayer. Accept our supplication and abolish the handwriting of our sins that is written against us, just as You tore it in this holy hour, by the cross of Your Only-Begotten Son, Jesus Christ, our Lord and Savior of our souls, this is by which you destroyed all the power of the enemy. Grant us, O God, a glorious time, a spotless conduct, and a peaceful life, so that we may please Your holy and worshipped name, and that, without falling into condemnation, we may stand before the fearful and just throne of Your Only-Begotten Son Jesus Christ our Lord, and that we, together with all Your saints, glorify You, our Father, who is without beginning, and the Son who is of one essence with You, and the Holy Spirit the Life-Giver, now and forever and unto the ages of all ages. Amen.

THE CONCLUSION OF EVERY HOUR
page 68

The Ninth Hour

(At this hour our Lord accepted the thief on the right to Paradise then died on the cross.)

INTRODUCTION TO EVERY HOUR

The Lord's Prayer	**Page 2**
The Thanksgiving prayer	**Page 4**
Psalm 50	**Page 6**

In the name of the Father, and the Son, and the Holy Spirit, one God. Amen.

Kyrie eleison. Lord have mercy, Lord have mercy, Lord bless us. Amen.

Glory to the Father, and to the Son, and to the Holy Spirit, now and forever and unto the ages of all ages. Amen.

The prayer of the Ninth Hour of the blessed day, we offer to Christ our King and our God, beseeching Him to forgive us our sins.

From the Psalms of our father David the prophet and the king, may his blessings be upon us all. Amen.

(1)   **PSALM 95**

Sing to the Lord a new song; sing to the Lord, all the earth. Sing to the Lord, bless His name: proclaim His salvation day to day.

Declare His glory among the Gentiles, and His wonders among all peoples. For the Lord is great, and greatly praised: He is fearful above all the gods. For all the gods of the nations are devils, but the Lord made the heavens. Majesty and splendor are before Him: holiness and great beauty are in His Holy.

Bring to the Lord, O the families of the Gentiles, bring to the Lord glory and honor. Bring to the Lord the glory of His name: carry offerings, and go into His court. Worship the Lord in His holy court:

let all the earth tremble before His face. Say among the nations, "The Lord reigned on a wood: for He has established the world that it shall not be moved: He will judge the peoples in righteousness."

Let the heavens rejoice, and the earth exult; let the sea be moved: and its fullness. The plains shall rejoice, and all things in them: then all the trees of the forest shall exult before the face of the Lord: for He is coming to judge the earth; He will judge the world in justice, and the peoples with His truth. ALLELUIA.

(2)   **PSALM 96**

The Lord reigns, let the earth exult, let the many islands rejoice. Cloud and darkness are round about Him; righteousness and judgement are the uprightness of His throne. Fire shall precede Him, and with a flame shall burn up His enemies who surround Him.

His lightings lightened the world; the earth saw, and trembled. The mountains melted like wax before the face of the Lord, before the face of the Lord of the whole earth. The heavens have declared His righteousness, and all the peoples have seen His glory. All those who worship graven images and boast in their idols shall be ashamed.

Worship Him all you His angels. Zion heard and rejoiced; and the daughters of Judea exulted, because of Your judgements, O Lord. For You are Lord most high over all the earth; You are greatly exalted above all the gods. You who love the Lord, hate evil; the Lord preserves the souls of His saints; He will deliver them from the hands of the sinners. Light has shined for the righteous, and gladness for the upright in their heart. Rejoice in the Lord, you righteous; and praise the remembrance of His holiness. ALLELUIA

(3)   **PSALM 97**

Sing to the Lord a new song; for the Lord has wrought wonderful works, His right hand and His holy arm, have wrought life for Him. The Lord has made known His salvation; before the nations He has revealed his righteousness. He has remembered His mercy to Jacob, and His truth to the house of Israel; the ends of all the earth have seen the salvation of our God. Shout to the Lord, all the earth; sing and exult, and sing psalms. Sing to the Lord with a harp, with a harp and a voice of psalm, with directed trumpets, and a sound of a trumpet of horn. Shout joyfully before the Lord King.

Let the sea be moved, and its fullness, the world and all who dwell in it. The rivers shall clap their hands together; and the mountains shall exult before the Lord. For He comes to judge the earth: He will judge the world with righteousness, and the nations with uprightness. ALLELUIA.

(4)   PSALM 98

The Lord reigned; let the people rage; He who sits upon the cherubim, let the earth be shaken. The Lord is great in Zion, and is high over all peoples. Let them confess His great name; for it is fearful and holy, and the King's honor loves the judgment. You have prepared uprightness, You have made judgment and justice in Jacob. Exalt the Lord our God, and worship at His footstool; for He is holy. Moses and Aaron among His priests, and Samuel among those who call upon His name; they called upon the Lord, and He heard them. He spoke to them in a pillar of cloud; for they kept His testimonies and the ordinances which He gave them. O Lord our God, You answered them; O God, You became for them a forgiver and an avenger over all their deeds. Exalt you the Lord our God, and worship at His holy mountain; for the Lord our God is holy. ALLELUIA.

(5)   PSALM 99

Shout joyfully to the Lord, all the earth. Serve the Lord with gladness; come into His presence with exultation. Know that the Lord Himself is our God; He made us, and not we ourselves; we are His people, and the sheep of His pasture.

Enter into His gates with thanksgiving, and His courts with praise; give thanks to Him, praise His name. For the Lord is good, His mercy is forever; and His truth is from generation to generation. ALLELUIA.

(6) **PSALM 100**

I will sing of mercy and judgment, to You, O Lord; I will sing a psalm, and I will have understanding in a blameless way. When will You come to me? I walked in the innocence of my heart, in the midst of my house. I have not set before my eyes any unlawful thing; I have hated transgressors. A perverse heart has not cleaved to me; I have not known the evil one, forasmuch as he turns away from me. He who secretly speaks against his neighbor, him I have driven from me: he who is proud in his eyes and haughty in heart, with him I have not eaten. My eyes were upon all the faithful of the land, that they might sit with me: he who walked in a blameless way, he ministered to me. The proud doer did not dwell in the midst of my house; the unjust speaker did not prosper before my eyes.

In the morning I slew all the sinners of the land, that I might wipe out from the city of the Lord all who work iniquity. ALLELUIA.

(7)   PSALM 109

The Lord said to my Lord, "Sit on My right hand, until I place Your enemies under Your feet." A rod of power, the Lord shall send out for You out of Zion: and You shall rule in the midst of Your enemies. With You is dominion in the day of Your power, in the splendor of the saints. From the womb before the morning star I have begotten You. The Lord has sworn and shall not repent: "You are the Priest forever, after the order of Melchizedek." The Lord is at Your right hand; He dashed kings in the day of His wrath. He shall judge among the nations. He shall fill them with dead bodies, He shall crush the heads of many on the earth. He shall drink of the brook in the way; therefore He shall lift up the head. ALLELUIA.

(8)   PSALM 110

I will confess You, O Lord, with my whole heart, in the council of the upright, and in their congregation. Great are the works of the Lord, examined are all His wills. Majesty and splendor are His works: and His righteousness endures forever and ever. He has made a remembrance of all His wonders: the Lord is merciful and compassionate. He has given food to those who fear Him: He shall remember His covenant forever. He has declared to His people the power of His works, to give them the inheritance of nations. The works of His hands are truth and justice: all His commandments are faithful: established forever and ever, made in truth and uprightness. He sent redemption to His people: He commanded His covenant forever: holy and fearful is His name. The fear of the Lord is the beginning of wisdom, and understanding is good to all who do according to it. His praise endures forever and ever. ALLELUIA.

(9)   **PSALM 111**

Blessed is the man who fears the Lord, and delights greatly in His commandments. His seed shall be mighty in the earth: the generation of the upright shall be blessed. Glory and riches shall be in His house; and His righteousness endures forever. To the upright, light has sprung up in the darkness. The Lord God is compassionate, merciful, and righteous.

A good man is he who pities and lends: he shall direct his words with truth. For he shall not be moved forever. The righteous shall be in everlasting remembrance. He shall not be afraid of any evil tidings: his heart is ready trusting the Lord. His heart is established, he shall not move, till he shall look upon his enemies. He has dispersed abroad; he has given to the poor; his righteousness endures forever and ever: his horn shall be exalted with honor. The sinner shall see and be angry, he shall gnash his teeth, and consume away: the desire of the sinner shall perish. ALLELUIA.

(10) **PSALM 112**

Praise the Lord, O the servants, praise the name of the Lord. Let the name of the Lord be blessed, from now and forever. From the risings of the sun to its settings, praise the name of the Lord. The Lord is high above all the nations; upon the heavens is His glory. Who is like the Lord our God? Who dwells in the high places, and looks upon the low things in heaven and on the earth: who lifts up a poor person from the earth, and raises up a needy person from the ash heap; to seat him with the princes, even with the princes of his people: who makes a barren woman in a house, rejoicing as a mother of children. ALLELUIA.

(11)   PSALM 114

I loved, because the Lord will hear the voice of my supplication. Because He has inclined His ear to me, I will call upon Him in all my days. The pains of death grasped me; the dangers of Hades have found me: I found affliction and sorrow. Then I called on the name of the Lord: "O Lord, deliver my soul." The Lord is merciful and righteous; and our God has mercy. The Lord preserves the infants: I was brought low, and He saved me. Return to your resting place, O my soul, for the Lord has dealt bountifully with you. He has delivered my soul from death, my eyes from tears, and my feet from falling. I shall please the Lord in the land of the living. ALLELUIA.

(12)   PSALM 115

I believed, therefore, I have spoken: I was exceedingly humbled. I said in my amazement, "Every man is a liar." What shall I render to the Lord for everything which He has done unto me? I shall take the cup of salvation, and call upon the name of the Lord. I will pay my vows to the Lord, in the presence of all His people. Precious in the sight of the Lord is the death of His saints. O Lord, I am Your servant; I am Your servant, and the son of Your handmaid: You have broken my bonds. I will sacrifice to You the sacrifice of praise, and will call upon the name of the Lord. I will pay my vows to the Lord in the presence of all His people, in the courts of the Lord's house, in the midst of Jerusalem. ALLELUIA.

THE HOLY GOSPEL ACCORDING TO ST. LUKE (CH. 9 : 10-17)

And the Apostles, when they had returned, told Him all that they had done. Then He took them, and went aside privately into a deserted place belonging to the city called Bethsaida. And the multitude, when they knew it, followed Him: and He received them, and spoke to them about the kingdom of God, and healed those who had need of healing. And when the day began to wear away, the twelve came, and said to Him, "Send the multitude away, that they may go into the towns and country round about, and lodge, and get provisions: for we are here in a deserted place." But He said unto them, "You give them to eat." And they said, "We have no more than five loaves and two fish; unless we go and buy food for all these people." For they were about five thousand men.

And He said to His disciples, "Make them sit down in groups of fifty." And they did so, and made them all sit down.

Then He took the five loaves and the two fish, and looking up to heaven, He blessed them, and broke, and gave to the disciples to set before the multitude.

And they ate, and were all filled, and twelve baskets of the remaining fragments were taken by them.

Glory to God forever. Amen.

LITANIES

(1) O You, Who tasted death in the flesh in the ninth hour for our sake, we the sinners, put to death our carnal lusts, O Christ, our God, and deliver us. Let my supplication draw close before You, O Lord; according to Your word give me understanding. Let my petition come before Your presence; according to Your word revive me. *(Doxa Patri ke Eioa ke Agio Pnevmati)*

(2) O You, who commended the spirit into the hands of the Father as You hung on the cross, in the ninth hour, and guided the Thief who was crucified with You into entering the Paradise, do not neglect me, O Good One, nor reject me, I, the lost one; but sanctify my soul and enlighten my understanding, and allow me to be a partaker of the grace of Your life-giving mysteries; that when I taste of Your benevolences, I offer You praise without lukewarmness, longing for Your splendor above all things, O Christ our Lord, and deliver us. *(Ke nin..)*

(3) O, You, who was born of the Virgin for our sake, and endured crucifixion, O Good One, and abolished death by Your death, and manifested resurrection by Your resurrection, O God, do not turn away from those whom You have created with Your own hands, but manifest, O Good One, Your love for mankind. Accept from Your mother an intercession on our behalf. Deliver, O Savior, a humble people. Do not leave us to the end, and do not forsake us forever. Do not break Your covenant, and do not take away from us your mercy, for the sake of Abraham, Your beloved, Isaac, Your servant, and Israel, Your saint. *(Ke nin ..)*

(4) When the Thief saw the Prince of Life hung on the cross, he said: "Had not the One Crucified with us been God Incarnate, the sun would not hide its rays, nor would the earth have quaked trembling. But O You, the Almighty One who endures all things, remember me, O Lord, when You come into Your kingdom." *(Doxa Patri ..)*

(5) O You, who accepted unto Him the confession of the Thief on the cross, accept us unto You, O Good One; we who deserve the sentence of death because of our sins. We all confess our sins with him, and acknowledging Your divinity, and cry out with him saying, "Remember us, O Lord, when You come into Your Kingdom." *(Ke nin ..)*

(6) When the mother saw the Lamb and Shepherd, the Savior of the world, hung on the Cross, she said while weeping, "The world rejoices in receiving salvation, while my heart burns as I look at Your crucifixion which You are enduring for the sake of all, my Son and my God."

Lord, hear us and have mercy on us and forgive us our sins. Amen.

Kyrie eleison, Lord have mercy (41 times)
HOLY HOLY HOLY   page 64
Our Father who art in Heaven...

ABSOLUTION

God, Father, the Father of our Lord, God and Savior, Jesus Christ, who, through His manifestation saved us and delivered us from the bondage of the enemy, we ask You, in His blessed and great name, turn our minds away from worldly cares and carnal lusts, to the remembrance of Your heavenly statutes; and reveal to us Your love for mankind, O Good One.

May our prayers at all times, and specially the prayer of this ninth hour, be favorably accepted by You. And grant us to walk worthy of the calling with which we were called, so that when we depart from this world, we may be counted with the worshippers worthy of the passions of Your Only-Begotten Son Jesus Christ, our Lord. Thus, we gain mercy, and forgiveness of our sins, and salvation with the choir of saints who truly pleased You since the beginning and forever. Lord, abolish for us the power of the adversary and all his evil armies, as Your Only-Begotten Son has trampled on them by the power of His life-giving cross. Accept us unto You, O our Lord, Jesus Christ, as You accepted the Thief at Your right, while You were hung on the cross. And shine upon us as You have shone upon those who were in the darkness of Hades, and restore us all to the paradise of joy. For You, our Master, are blessed God, and unto You is due all the glory, honor, majesty, dominion, and worship, with Your good Father and the Holy Spirit, forever. Amen.

THE CONCLUSION OF EVERY HOUR
page 68

The Eleventh Hour

(At this hour our Lord's body was taken down off the cross to be buried.)

INTRODUCTION TO EVERY HOUR

The Lord's Prayer	**Page 2**
The Thanksgiving prayer	**Page 4**
Psalm 50	**Page 6**

In the name of the Father, and the Son, and the Holy Spirit, one God. Amen.

Kyrie eleison. Lord have mercy, Lord have mercy, Lord bless us. Amen.

Glory to the Father, and to the Son, and to the Holy Spirit, now and forever and unto the ages of all ages. Amen.

The prayer of the Eleventh Hour of the blessed day, we offer to Christ our King and our God, beseeching Him to forgive us our sins.

From the Psalms of our father David the prophet and the king, may his blessings be upon us all. Amen.

(1)   PSALM 116

Praise the Lord, all you nations: let all the peoples praise Him. For His mercy has been established upon us, and the truth of the Lord endures forever. ALLELUIA.

(2)   PSALM 117

Give thanks to the Lord; for He is good: for His mercy endures forever. Let now the house of Israel say that He is good: for His mercy endures forever. Let the house of Aaron say that He is good: for His mercy endures forever. Let now all who fear the Lord say that He is good: for His mercy endures forever. I called on the Lord in my affliction: and He answered me, and brought me into a broad place. The Lord is my helper; and I shall not fear what man will do to me. The Lord is my helper; and I shall look down upon my own enemies. It is better to trust in the Lord than to trust in man. It is better to hope in the Lord, than to hope in princes. All the nations surrounded me: and in the name of the Lord I drove them away. They surrounded me and went around me: and in the name of the Lord I drove them away. They surrounded me as bees around a honeycomb, and they burst as fire among thorns: and in the name of the Lord I drove them away. I was pushed, that I might fall: but the Lord helped me. My strength and my praise is the Lord, and He has become unto me a salvation. The voice of exultation and salvation is in the dwellings of the righteous: the right hand of the Lord has wrought mightily. The right hand of the Lord has exalted me: the right hand of the Lord has wrought powerfully. I shall not die, but live, and recount the works of the Lord. With chastisement the Lord has chastened me: and has not given me up to death. Open to me the gates of righteousness: that I will go into them, and praise the Lord. This is the gate of the Lord: the righteous shall enter into it. I will praise You, O Lord, because You have answered me, and have become unto me a salvation. The stone which the builders rejected has become the head of the corner. This has been done by the Lord; and it is wonderful in our eyes.

This is the day which the Lord has made: let us rejoice and be glad in it. O Lord, save us: O Lord, ease our ways. Blessed is He who comes in the name of the Lord: we have blessed you from the house of the Lord. God the Lord has shined upon us: ordain a feast with those that reach the horns of the altar. You are my God, and I will give thanks to You: You are my God, and I will exalt You. I will give thanks to You, O Lord, for You have heard me, and have become unto me a salvation. Give thanks to the Lord; for He is good: for His mercy endures forever. ALLELUIA.

(3)   **PSALM 119**

In my own affliction I cried to You, O Lord, and You heard me. O Lord, You shall deliver my soul from unjust lips, and from a deceitful tongue. What should be given to you, and what should be added to you, a crafty tongue?! The weapons of the mighty are sharpened with coals of the desert! Woe to me, that my sojourning is prolonged; I have lived among the dwellings of Kedar. My soul has long been a sojourner; I was peaceable among those who hated peace; when I spoke to them. they warred against me without a cause. ALLELUIA.

(4)   **PSALM 120**

I lifted up my eyes to the mountains, from where my help shall come. My help shall come from the Lord, who made the heaven and the earth. He will not let your foot be moved; and your keeper will not slumber. Behold, He who keeps Israel shall not slumber nor sleep. The Lord shall keep you: the Lord shall cast a shelter upon your right hand. The sun shall not burn you by day, neither the moon by night. The Lord shall preserve you from every evil: the Lord shall keep your soul. The Lord shall keep your coming in and your going out, from this time and forever. ALLELUIA.

(5)   PSALM 121

I was glad for those who said to me, "We will go into the house of the Lord." Our feet stood in the courts of Jerusalem, Jerusalem which is built as a city that is closely compacted together. For there the tribes went up, the tribes of the Lord, as a testimony for Israel, confessing the name of the Lord. For there are set thrones for judgment, even thrones for the house of David. Ask for the things which are for the peace of Jerusalem: and for the prosperity to those who love you. Let peace be within your strength, and prosperity in your heavy towers. For the sake of my brothers and my companions, I have indeed spoken peace concerning you. Because of the house of the Lord our God, I have diligently sought good things for you. ALLELUIA.

(6) **PSALM 122**

Unto You I have lifted up my eyes, O You who dwell in heaven. Behold as the eyes of servants are unto to the hands of their masters, and as the eyes of a maidservant to the hands of her mistress; so our eyes are toward the Lord our God until He has pity on us. Have mercy on us, O Lord, have mercy on us: for we are exceedingly filled with contempt. And our soul has been exceedingly filled: give the reproach to those who prosper, and contempt to the proud. ALLELUIA.

(7) **PSALM 123**

If it had not been that the Lord is among us, let Israel say; if it had not been that the Lord is among us when men rose up against us, then they would have swallowed us up alive, when their wrath was kindled against us. Then the water would have drowned us. Our soul would have gone under the raging flood; then our soul would have gone under the unlimited water. Blessed be the Lord, who has not given us for a prey to their teeth. Our soul has been delivered as a sparrow from the snare of the hunters. The snare has broken, and we were delivered. Our help is in the name of the Lord, who made heaven and earth. ALLELUIA.

(8)   PSALM 124

Those who trust in the Lord are as Mount Zion:
he who dwells in Jerusalem shall never be
moved. Mountains are round about her, and the
Lord is round about His people, from this time
and forever. For the Lord shall not allow the rod
of sinners to be upon the lot of the righteous; lest
the righteous might stretch forth their hands to
iniquity. Do good, O Lord, to those who are
good, and to those who are upright in their heart.
But those who turn to stumbles, the Lord will
banish with the workers of iniquity; peace be
upon Israel. ALLELUIA.

(9)   PSALMS 125

When the Lord brought back the captivity of
Zion, we became as those who were comforted.
Then our mouth was filled with joy, and our
tongue with exultation. Then they shall say
among the Gentiles, "The Lord has done great
things among them." The Lord has done great
things for us, we became joyful.

O Lord, You shall bring back our captivity, as
the streams in the south. Those who sow in tears
shall reap in joy. They went on and wept as they
were carrying their seeds; but they shall surely

come with exultation, carrying their sheaves. ALLELUIA.

(10)   PSALMS 126

Unless the Lord builds the house, those who build it have labored in vain. Unless the Lord guards the city, the watchmen have watched in vain. It is vain for you to rise early: rise up after your sitting, you who eat the bread of grief; while He gives sleep to His beloved. Behold, children are the inheritance of the Lord, the reward of the fruit of the womb. As arrows in the hand of a mighty man, so are the children of one's youth. Blessed is the man who has his quiver full of them; they shall not be ashamed when they speak with their enemies in the gates. ALLELUIA.

(11)   PSALMS 127

Blessed are all who fear the Lord; who walk in his ways. You shall eat the fruit of your labors: you shall be blessed, and goodness shall be unto you.

Your wife shall be as a fruitful vine on the sides of your house, your children as young olive-plants round about your table. Behold, thus shall the man be blessed, who fears the Lord. The Lord shall bless you out of Zion; and you shall see the good things of Jerusalem all the days of your life. And you shall see the children of your children. Peace be upon Israel. ALLELUIA.

(12)   PSALMS 128

Many times they have warred against me from my youth, let Israel now say. Many times they have warred against me from my youth, and yet they have not prevailed against me. The sinners scourged me on my back, and prolonged their iniquity. The Lord is righteous; He has broken the necks of sinners.

Let all who hate Zion be put to shame and turned back. Let them be as the grass of the house-tops, which withers before it is plucked up, with which the reaper does not fill his hand, nor he who gathers up sheaves, his bosom. Neither do they who pass by say, "The blessing of the Lord be upon you, we have blessed you in the name of the Lord." ALLELUIA.

THE HOLY GOSPEL ACCORDING TO ST. LUKE (CH. 4 : 38-41)

And He arose out of the synagogue, and entered into Simon's house. And Simon's wife's mother was taken with a great fever; and they requested Him concerning her. And He stood over her, and rebuked the fever; and it left her: and immediately she arose and served them. When the sun was setting, all those who had any sick with divers diseases brought them unto Him; and He laid His hands on every one of them, and healed them. And devils also came out of many, crying out, and saying, "You are Christ, the Son of God!" And He, rebuking them, did not allow them to speak: for they knew that He was Christ. Glory to God forever. Amen.

LITANIES

(1) If the righteous one is scarcely saved, where shall I, the sinner, appear? The burden and heat of the day I did not endure because of the weakness of my humanity. But, O merciful God, count me with the fellows of the eleventh hour. For, behold, in iniquities I was conceived, and in sins my mother bore me. Therefore, I do not dare to lift up my eyes to Heaven; but rather, I rely on the abundance of Your mercy and love for mankind, crying out and saying, "God, forgive me, a sinner, and have mercy on me." *(Doxa Patri ..)*

(2) Hasten, O Savior, to open to me the fatherly bosoms, for I wasted my life in pleasures and lusts, and the day has passed by me and vanished. Therefore, now I rely on the richness of Your never-ending compassion. So, then, do not forsake a submissive heart which is in need of your mercy. For unto You I cry, O Lord, humbly, "Father, I have sinned against Heaven and before You, and I am no longer worthy to be called Your son, so make me as one of Your hired servants." *(Ke nin ..)*

(3) Every iniquity I did with prudence and activity, and every sin I committed with eagerness and diligence, and of all torment and judgment I am worthy. Therefore, prepare for me the ways of repentance, O Lady the Virgin; for to you I appeal, and through you I seek intercession, and upon you I call to help me, lest I might be put to shame. And when my soul departs my body attend to me, and defeat the conspiracy of the enemies, and shut the gates of Hades, lest they might swallow my soul, O you, blameless bride of the true Bridegroom.

Lord, hear us and have mercy on us and forgive us our sins. Amen.

Kyrie eleison, Lord have mercy (41 times)
HOLY HOLY HOLY   page 64
Our Father who art in Heaven...

ABSOLUTION

We thank You, our compassionate king, for You have granted us to pass this day in peace, and brought us to the evening thankfully, and made us worthy to behold daylight until evening. Lord, accept our glorification which is offered now, and save us from the trickeries of the adversary, and abolish all the snares which are set against us. Grant us, in this coming night, peace without pain, or anxiety, or unrest, or illusion; so that we may pass it in peace and chastity, and rise up for praises and prayers. And thus, at all times and everywhere, we glorify

Your holy name in everything, together with the Father, who is incomprehensible and without beginning, and the Holy Spirit, the Life-Giver, Who is in one essence with You, now and at all times, and unto the ages of all ages. Amen.

THE CONCLUSION OF EVERY HOUR
page 68

The Twelfth Hour

(At this hour our Lord's body was placed in the tomb. It also represents the end of man's life.)

INTRODUCTION TO EVERY HOUR

The Lord's Prayer	**Page 2**
The Thanksgiving prayer	**Page 4**
Psalm 50	**Page 6**

In the name of the Father, and the Son, and the Holy Spirit, one God. Amen.

Kyrie eleison. Lord have mercy, Lord have mercy, Lord bless us. Amen.

Glory to the Father, and to the Son, and to the Holy Spirit, now and forever and unto the ages of all ages. Amen.

The prayer of the Twelfth Hour of the blessed day, we offer to Christ our King and our God, beseeching Him to forgive us our sins.

From the Psalms of our father David the prophet and the king, may his blessings be upon us all. Amen.

(1)   PSALM 129

Out of the depths I have cried to You, O Lord. O Lord, hear my voice: let Your ears be attentive to the voice of my supplication. If You, O Lord, should mark iniquities, O Lord, who shall stand? For through You is forgiveness. For Your name's sake I have waited for You, O Lord. My soul has waited for Your law. My soul has hoped in the Lord, from the morning watch till night. From the morning watch, let Israel hope in the Lord. For with the Lord is mercy, and great is His redemption; and He shall redeem Israel from all his iniquities. ALLELUIA.

(2)   PSALM 130

O Lord, my heart was not exalted, neither have my eyes been haughtily raised: neither have I walked in great matters, nor in wonders greater than me. If I have not humbled myself, but raised my soul, as a weaned child with his mother, so is the recompense upon my soul. Let Israel hope in the Lord, from now and forever. ALLELUIA.

(3)   **PSALM 131**

Lord, remember David and all his meekness:
how he swore to the Lord, and vowed to the God
of Jacob, saying, "I will not go into the dwelling
of my house, or go up to the bed of my couch; I
will not give sleep to my eyes, nor slumber to
my eyelids, nor rest to my temples, until I find a
place for the Lord, and a dwelling place for the
God of Jacob. Behold, we heard of it in
Ephratha; we found it in the fields of the wood.
Let us enter into His dwelling, and worship at
the place where His feet stood.

Arise, O Lord, into Your rest; You, and the ark
of Your holy place. Your priests shall clothe
themselves with righteousness; and Your
righteous shall exult. For the sake of Your
servant David, do not turn away Your face
from Your anointed. The Lord has sworn in
truth to David, and He will not turn from it, "Of
the fruit of your loins I will set upon your
throne. If your children keep My covenant and
My testimonies which I will teach them, their
children also will sit upon your throne forever."
For the Lord has selected Zion, He has chosen
her a dwelling for Himself: "This is My resting
place forever. Here I will dwell; for I have
desired it. In blessing I shall bless her hunting.

Her poor I shall satisfy with bread. Her priests I shall clothe with salvation; and her saints with rejoicing shall rejoice. There I shall raise a horn to David. I have prepared a lamp for My anointed. His enemies I shall clothe with shame, and My holiness shall flourish upon Him." ALLELUIA.

(4)   PSALM 132

Behold! What is so good, or what so pleasant, as for brothers dwelling together? It is as ointment upon the head, that came down upon beard, the beard of Aaron that came down to the fringe of his clothing; as the dew of Aermon, that comes down upon the mountain of Zion: for there the Lord commanded the blessing and the life forever. ALLELUIA.

(5)   PSALM 133

Behold, bless the Lord, O you the servants of the Lord, who stand in the house of the Lord, in the courts of the house of our God. In the nights lift up your hands unto the Holies, and bless the Lord. The Lord shall bless you out of Zion, He who made heaven and earth. ALLELUIA.

(6)   **PSALM 136**

By the rivers of Babylon, there we sat and wept when we remembered Zion. We hung our harps on the willows in the midst of it. For there those who had taken us captive asked of us the words of a song; and those who had carried us away asked a hymn, saying, "Sing us one of the songs of Zion." How will we sing the Lord's song in a strange land? If I forget you, O Jerusalem, I shall forget my right hand. My tongue shall cling to my throat, if I did not remember you; if I did not prefer Jerusalem as the head of my joy. Remember, O Lord, the children of Edom in the day of Jerusalem; who said, "Tear it down, tear it down, even to its foundations." Wretched daughter of Babylon! Blessed is he who will reward you with the reward you have given us. Blessed is he who will seize and bury your infants by the rock. ALLELUIA.

(7)   **PSALM 137**

I will confess You, O Lord, with my whole heart, for You have heard all the words of my mouth. Before the angels I will chant to You. I will worship toward Your holy temple, and confess Your name, on account of Your mercy and Your truth; for You have magnified Your holy name above all. The day in which I call upon You, hear me speedily; You shall exceedingly look upon my soul with power.

Let all the kings of the earth, O Lord, confess You; for they have heard all the words of Your mouth. And let them sing in the ways of the Lord; for great is the glory of the Lord. The Lord is high, and He regards the lowly; and He knows the existing things from afar off. If I walk in the midst of affliction, You shall revive me; You have stretched forth Your hands against the wrath of enemies, and Your right hand has saved me. O Lord, You shall reward on my behalf: Your mercy, O Lord, endures forever: do not overlook the works of Your hands. ALLELUIA.

(8)   PSALM 140

O Lord, I have cried to You, hear me. Attend to the voice of my supplication when I cry to You. Let my prayer be set forth before You as incense, and the lifting up of my hands as an evening sacrifice. O Lord, set a watch on my mouth and a strong door for my lips. Do not incline my heart to words of evil, to employ excuses for sins with men who work iniquity; and I shall not agree with their choices.

The righteous shall chasten me with mercy, and reprove me: but do not let the oil of the sinner anoint my head: for yet my prayer also is in their pleasures. Their mighty ones have been swallowed up near the rock: they shall hear my words, for they are delightful. As a lump of earth, they are broken upon the ground, their bones have been scattered at Hades. For my eyes are to You, O Lord: O Lord, I have hoped in You; do not take away my soul. Keep me from the snare which they have set for me, and from the stumbling blocks of those who work iniquity. Sinners shall fall by their own net: I am alone until iniquity passes by. ALLELUIA.

(9)   PSALM 141

With my voice to the Lord I cried; with my voice to the Lord I made supplication. I will pour out before Him my supplication. My affliction I will pour out before Him, when my spirit was fainting within me, and You knew my paths. In the way in which I was walking, they hid a snare for me. I looked on my right hand, and beheld, for there was no one who noticed me. Refuge failed me, and there was no one who cared for my soul. I cried unto You, O Lord, and said, "You are my hope, my portion in the land of the living. Attend to my supplication, for I am brought very low;

deliver me from those who persecute me, for they are stronger than me. Bring my soul out of prison, that I may confess Your name, O Lord. The righteous wait for me until You reward me." ALLELUIA.

(10)   PSALM 145

Praise the Lord, O my soul. I will praise the Lord in my life. I will sing praises to my God as long as I exist. Do not trust in the princes, nor in the children of men, in whom there is no salvation. Their spirit shall go forth, and they shall return to their earth. In that day all their thoughts shall perish. Blessed is he whose helper is the God of Jacob, whose hope is in the Lord his God: who made heaven and earth, the sea and all things in them; who keeps truth forever: who executes judgment for the oppressed, who gives food to the hungry.

The Lord looses the bound; the Lord sets up the broken down. The Lord gives wisdom to the blind; the Lord loves the righteous. the Lord preserves the strangers; He accepts the orphan and widow: but He will destroy the way of sinners. The Lord shall reign forever, and your God, O Zion, from generation to generation. ALLELUIA.

(11)   PSALM 146

Praise the Lord, for a psalm is good; let praise be sweet unto our God.

The Lord builds up Jerusalem; and He will gather together the dispersed of Israel. He heals the broken-hearted, and binds up all their fractures. He numbers the multitudes of stars, and calls them all by names.

Great is the Lord, and great is His strength; His understanding is infinite. The Lord lifts up the meek, but brings sinners down to the ground.

Begin the song to the Lord with thanksgiving; sing praises to our God on the harp: He who covers the heaven with clouds; who prepares rain for the earth; who causes grass to spring up on the mountains, and green herb for the service of men; who gives food to the cattle, and to the young ravens that call upon Him.

He will not take pleasure in the strength of a horse, nor will He be well-pleased with the legs of man. The Lord will take pleasure in those who fear Him, and in those who hope in His mercy. ALLELUIA.

(12)   PSALM 147

Praise the Lord, O Jerusalem; praise your God, O Zion: for He has strengthened the bars of your gates.

He has blessed your children within you. He makes your borders peaceful, and fills you with the fatness of wheat.

He sends His word to the earth: His word runs swiftly.

He gives snow like wool: He scatters the mist like ashes.

He casts out His ice like morsels: who will be able to stand before His frost? He will send out His word, and melt them. His wind will blow, and the waters shall flow.

He declares His word to Jacob, His ordinances and judgments to Israel.

He has not done so with every nation; and He has not revealed to them His judgments. ALLELUIA.

THE HOLY GOSPEL ACCORDING TO ST. LUKE (CH. 2 : 25-32)

And behold, there was a man in Jerusalem, whose name was Simeon; and this man was just and devout, waiting for the consolation of Israel; and the Holy Spirit was upon him. And it had been revealed to him by the Holy Spirit that he would not see death before he had seen Christ the Lord. So he came by the Spirit into the temple. And when the parents brought in the Child Jesus, to do for Him according to the custom of the law, he took Him up in his arms and blessed God, and said: "Lord, now You are letting Your servant depart in peace, according to Your word; for my eyes have seen Your salvation, which You have prepared before the face of all peoples, a light for the revelation to the Gentiles, and the glory of Your people Israel." Glory be to God forever. Amen.

LITANIES

(1) Behold, I am about to stand before the Just Judge terrified and trembling because of my many sins. For a life spent in pleasures deserves condemnation. But repent, O my soul, so long as you dwell on earth, for inside the grave, dust does not praise and in death, no one remembers, neither in Hades, does anyone give thanks. Therefore arise from the slumber of laziness, and entreat the Savior, repenting and saying, "God, have mercy on me and save me." *(Doxa Patri ..)*

(2) If life were everlasting, and this world ever-existing, you would have an excuse, O my soul. But if your wicked deeds and ugly evils were exposed before the Just Judge, what answer would you give while you are lying on the bed of sins, negligent in disciplining the flesh!? O Christ our God, before Your awesome seat of judgment I am terrified, and before Your council of judgment I submit, and from the Light of Your divine radiance I tremble, I, the wretched and defiled, who lies on my bed, negligent in my life. But I take example of the Publican, beating my chest and saying, "O God, forgive me and have mercy on me, a sinner." *(Ke nin ..)*

(3) O Holy Virgin, overshadow your servant with your instant help, and keep the waves of evil thoughts away from me, and raise up my ailing soul for prayer and vigil, for it has gone into a deep sleep. For you are a capable, compassionate and helpful mother, the bearer of the Fountain of Life, my King and my God, Jesus Christ, my hope.

GRACIOUSLY ACCORD, O LORD

Graciously accord, O Lord, to keep us this night without sin. Blessed are You, O Lord, God of our fathers, and exceedingly blessed, and glorified be Your name forever. Amen.

Let Your mercy, O Lord, be upon us, according to our hope in You; for the eyes of everyone wait upon You, for You give them their food in due season. Hear us, O God, our Savior, the hope of all the regions of the earth. And You, O Lord, keep us safe from this generation and forever. Amen.

Blessed are You, O Lord; teach me Your statutes. Blessed are You, O Lord; make me to understand Your commandments. Blessed are You, O Lord; enlighten me with Your righteousness. Your mercy, O Lord, endures forever. Despise not, O Lord, the works of Your hands. You have been my refuge from generation to generation.

I asked the Lord and said, "Have mercy on me, heal my soul; for I have sinned against You." Lord, I have fled unto You, save me, and teach me to do Your will, for You are my God, and with You is the fountain of life. In Your light shall we see light. Let Your mercy come unto those who know You, and Your righteousness unto the upright in heart. To You belongs blessing. To You belongs praise. To You belongs glory, O Father, Son and Holy Spirit, existing from the beginning, now, and forever and ever. Amen. It is good to confess unto the Lord, and to sing praises unto Your name, O Most High; to show forth Your mercy every morning, and Your righteousness every night.

THE TRISAGION   **page 56**
INTRODUCTION TO THE CREED **page 60**
THE ORTHODOX CREED   **page 60**
Kyrie eleison, Lord have mercy (41 times)
HOLY HOLY HOLY   **page 64**
Our Father who art in Heaven…

ABSOLUTION

Lord, all our sins which we committed against You in this day, whether in deeds or in words or in thoughts or through all senses, please remit and forgive us, for the sake of Your holy name, as You are Good and Lover of mankind. God, grant us a peaceful night and a sleep free from all anxiety. And send us an angel of peace to protect us from every evil, and every affliction, and every temptation of the enemy; through the Grace, compassion and love of mankind of Your Only-Begotten Son, our Lord, God and Savior Jesus Christ, to Whom is due, with You and with the Holy Spirit, the Life-Giver Who is of one essence with You, all glory, honor and dominion, now and forever and unto the ages of all ages. Amen.

THE CONCLUSION OF EVERY HOUR
page 68

The Veil

(This prayer concerns monks.)

INTRODUCTION TO EVERY HOUR

In the name of the Father, and the Son, and the Holy Spirit, one God. Amen.

Kyrie eleison. Lord have mercy, Lord have mercy, Lord bless us. Amen.

Glory to the Father, and to the Son, and to the Holy Spirit, now and forever and unto the ages of all ages. Amen.

The prayer of the Veil, we offer to Christ our King and our God, beseeching Him to forgive us our sins.

From the Psalms of our father David the prophet and the king, may his blessings be upon us all. Amen.

Psalm	Page	Beginning of the Psalm
4	18	When I cried out,
6	22	O Lord, do not rebuke me
12	28	How long, O Lord,
15	30	Keep me, O Lord;
24	34	To You, O Lord,
26	38	The Lord is my light
66	42	God shall pity us,
69	42	O God, be mindful
22	72	The Lord is He
29	80	I will exalt You
42	86	Judge me, O Lord
56	106	Have mercy upon me
85	118	Incline Your ear, O Lord
90	122	He who dwells
96	140	The Lord reigns
109	148	The Lord said to my Lord
114	154	I loved, because
115	156	I believed, therefore
120	174	I lifted up my eyes
128	184	Many times
129	196	Out of the depths

Psalm	Page	Beginning of the Psalm
130	196	O Lord, my heart
131	198	Lord, remember David
132	200	Behold! What is so good
133	200	Behold, bless the Lord
136	202	By the rivers of Babylon
140	204	O Lord, I have cried
145	208	Praise the Lord, O my soul
118	262	Paragraph 20, 21, 22

THE HOLY GOSPEL ACCORDING TO ST. JOHN (CH. 6 : 15-23)

When Jesus therefore perceived that they would come and take Him by force, to make Him a king, He departed again into a mountain Himself alone. And when evening came, His disciples went down to the sea, and entered into a ship, and went over the sea toward Capernaum. And it was now dark, and Jesus had not come to them. And the sea arose by reason of a great wind that blew. So when they had rowed about three or four miles, they saw Jesus walking on the sea, and drawing near to the ship: and they were afraid. But He said to them, It is I; do not be afraid. Then they willingly received Him into the ship: and immediately the ship was at the land where they were going.

The day following, the people who stood on the other side of the sea saw that there was no other boat there, except that one which His disciples were entered, and that Jesus went not with His disciples into the boat, but that His disciples were gone away alone. However, there came other boats from Tiberias near the place where they ate bread, after the Lord had given thanks. Glory to God forever. Amen.

LITANIES

(1) Lord, You know the alertness of my enemies, and as for my weakness, You are aware of it, My Creator. Therefore, I, hereby, place my soul into Your Hands. So cover me with the wings of Your goodness, lest I might sleep till death. Enlighten my eyes by the greatness of Your sayings, and raise me up at all times for Your glorification, for You alone are good and lover of mankind. *(Doxa Patri ...)*

(2) Lord, Your Judgment is dreadful; when men shall be rushed, the angels shall stand, the books shall be opened, the deeds shall be revealed, and the thoughts examined. What a Judgment mine will be, I who am entangled by sin?! Who would quench the flames of fire about me?! Who would enlighten my darkness, unless You, Lord?! Have mercy on me, for You are compassionate to mankind. *(Ke nin ...)*

(3) O *Theotokos,* because we have put our trust in you, we shall not be put to shame, but shall be saved. And because we have attained your help and intercession, O pure and perfect one, we shall not fear, but shall drive out our enemies and shall disperse them. And, in all, we take your great help to protect us as if with a shield. We ask and entreat you, crying, O *Theotokos,* to save us by your intercessions, and raise us up from the dark sleep, in order to powerfully glorify God Who took flesh from you.

THE TRISAGION	**page 56**
INTRODUCTION TO THE CREED	**page 60**
THE ORTHODOX CREED	**page 60**
Kyrie eleison, Lord have mercy (41 times)	

HOLY HOLY HOLY page 64
Our Father who art in Heaven...

ABSOLUTION

O Lord and Master, Jesus Christ our God, grant us rest in our sleep, repose of our bodies, and purity of our souls, and protect us from the darkness of devastating sin. May the pangs of pain subside, and the heat of the flesh calm down, and the turmoil of the body come to an end. Grant us an alert mind, a humble thought, a life full of virtue, and a pure and undefiled bed. Raise us up for the night and morning praises, steadfast in Your commandments, keeping in ourselves, at all times, the thought of Your judgments. Grant us to praise You the whole night; blessing Your holy name full of glory and splendor, with Your good Father, and the Holy Spirit, the Life-Giver, now and at all times and unto the ages of all ages. Amen.

THE CONCLUSION OF EVERY HOUR
page 68

Midnight Prayer – First Watch

(It reminds us with the second coming of our Lord Jesus Christ.)

INTRODUCTION TO EVERY HOUR	
The Lord's Prayer	**Page 2**
The Thanksgiving prayer	**Page 4**
Psalm 50	**Page 6**

♦ Arise, you, O children of the light, to praise the Lord of Hosts, that He may grant us the salvation of our souls. When we stand in the flesh before You, take away from our minds the sleep of forgetfulness, and grant us alertness, in order that we understand how to stand up before You at the time of prayer, and send up to You the appropriate doxology, and win the forgiveness of our many sins. *(Zoxasi Philanthrope…Glory be to You, the Lover of mankind.)*

♦ Behold, bless the Lord, O you the servants of the Lord, who stand in the house of the Lord, in the courts of the house of our God. In the nights lift up your hands unto the Holies, and bless the Lord. The Lord shall bless you out of Zion, He who made heaven and earth. *(Zoxasi Philanthrope…Glory be to You, the Lover of mankind.)*

♦ Let my supplication come near before You; give me understanding according to Your word. Let my petition come before You; revive me according to Your word. Let my lips flow with praise, when You have taught me Your ordinances. Let my tongue speak of Your words; for all Your commandments are righteous. Let Your hand be for saving me; for I have desired Your commandments. I have longed for Your salvation, O Lord; and Your law is my meditation. My soul shall live, and praise You; and Your judgments shall help me. I have gone astray like a lost sheep; seek Your servant; for I have not forgotten Your commandments.

Glory to the Father, and to the Son, and to the Holy Spirit, now and forever and unto the ages of all ages. Amen. Glory to the Father, and to the Son, and to the Holy Spirit, now and forever and unto the ages of all ages, Amen. Glory to You O the good and lover of mankind. Hail to Your mother the Virgin and to all Your Saints. Glory to You, O Holy Trinity; have mercy upon us.

Let God arise, and let His enemies be dispersed; and let all who hate His holy name flee before His face. But let Your people be in blessing, thousands of thousands, and ten thousand times ten thousands, doing Your will. O Lord, You shall open my lips; and my mouth shall declare Your praise. Amen. **ALLELUIA**

THE FIRST WATCH

The praise of the First Watch of the blessed Midnight Hour, we offer unto Christ our King and our God, beseeching Him to forgive us our sins.

From the Psalms of our father David the prophet and the king, may his blessings be upon us all. Amen.

Psalm	Page	
3	18	O Lord, why have they
6	22	O Lord, do not rebuke me
12	28	How long, O Lord
69	42	O God, be mindful
85	118	Incline Your ear, O Lord
90	122	He who dwells
116	170	Praise the Lord
117	170	Give thanks to the Lord

PSALM 118

(1) Blessed are the blameless in the way, who walk in the law of the Lord. Blessed are they who search out His testimonies: seeking Him with their whole heart. For they who work iniquity have not desired to walk in His ways. You have commanded that Your commandments be diligently kept. O that my ways were directed to keep Your ordinances! Then I shall not be ashamed, when I look on all Your commandments. I will give thanks to You, O Lord, with uprightness of my heart, when I have learned the judgments of Your righteousness. I will keep Your ordinances: do not exceedingly forsake me! *(Zoxasi..)*

(2) Wherewith shall a young man straighten his way? by keeping Your words. With my whole heart I have sought You: do not cast me away from Your commandments. I have hidden Your words in my heart, that I might not sin against You. Blessed are You, O Lord: teach me Your ordinances. With my lips I have declared all the judgments of Your mouth. I have delighted in the way of Your testimonies, as much as in all richness. I shall speak of Your commandments, and consider Your ways. I will meditate on Your ordinances, and I shall not forget Your words. *(Zoxasi..)*

(3) Render a reward to Your servant: so I shall live, and keep Your words. Unveil my eyes, and I shall perceive wondrous things out of Your law. I am a stranger upon the earth: do not hide Your commandments from me. My soul has longed to desire Your judgments at all times. You have rebuked the proud: cursed are those who turn aside from Your commandments. Remove from me the reproach and the contempt; for I have sought out Your testimonies. For princes sat and spoke against me: but Your servant was meditating on Your ordinances. For Your testimonies are my meditation, and Your ordinances are my counsels. *(Zoxasi..)*

(4) My soul has cleaved to the ground; revive me according to Your word. I declared Your ways, and You heard me: teach me Your ordinances. Instruct me in Your ordinances, and make known to me the way of Your righteousness; and I will meditate on Your wondrous works. My soul has slumbered from sorrow; strengthen me with Your words. Remove from me the way of iniquity; and be merciful to me by Your law. I have chosen the way of truth; and have not forgotten Your judgments. I have cleaved to Your testimonies, O Lord; do not put me to shame. I ran the way of Your commandments, when You enlarged my heart. *(Zoxasi..)*

(5) Set before me, O Lord, a law in the way of Your ordinances, and I will seek it out every time. Give me understanding, and I shall search out Your law, and shall keep it with my whole heart. Guide me in the path of Your commandments; for in this I have delighted. Incline my heart to Your testimonies, and not to covetousness. Turn away my eyes that I may not behold vanity: revive me in Your ways. Set Your word with Your servant in Your fear. Take away from me the reproach which I have feared: for Your judgments are sweet. Behold, I have desired Your commandments: revive me in Your righteousness. *(Zoxasi..)*

(6) Let Your mercy come upon me, O Lord; and Your salvation, according to Your word. So I shall answer with a word those who reproach me: for I have trusted in Your words. Do not take the word of truth exceedingly out of my mouth; for I have hoped in Your judgments. And I will keep Your law every time, forever and ever. I walked also at large: for I sought out Your commandments. And I spoke of Your testimonies before the kings, and was not ashamed. And I meditated on Your commandments, those which I loved exceedingly. And I lifted up my hands up to Your commandments which I exceedingly loved; and I meditated upon Your ordinances. *(Zoxasi..)*

(7) Remember Your words to Your servant, in which You have made me hope. This has comforted me in my affliction: for Your word is that which has revived me. The proud have transgressed exceedingly; but I did not incline away from Your law. I remembered Your judgments from the beginning, O Lord; and was comforted. Despair took hold of me, because of the sinners who forsook Your law. Your ordinances were songs for me in the place of my sojourning. I remembered Your name, O Lord, in the night, and kept Your law. This came unto me, because I sought Your ordinances. *(Zoxasi..)*

(8) You are my portion, O Lord: I said that I would keep Your commandments. I entreated Your face with my whole heart: have mercy on me according to Your word, for I meditated on Your ways, and turned my feet to Your testimonies. I prepared myself, and was not troubled, to keep Your commandments. The bonds of sinners entrapped me: but I did not forget Your law. At midnight I usually arise, to give thanks to You for the judgments of Your righteousness. I am the companion of all who fear You, and of all who keep Your commandments. O Lord, the earth is filled of Your mercy: teach me Your ordinances. *(Zoxasi..)*

(9) You have done good with Your servant, O Lord, according to Your word. Teach me kindness, and instruction, and knowledge: for I have believed Your commandments. Before I was humbled, I became lazy; therefore I have kept Your word. Sweet are You, O Lord; and in Your goodness teach me Your ordinances. The injustice of the proud has been multiplied against me: but I shall search out Your commandments with all my heart. Their heart has been curdled like milk; but I have meditated on Your law. It is good for me that You have humbled me; that I might learn Your ordinances. The law of Your mouth is better to me than thousands of gold and silver. *(Zoxasi..)*

(10) Your hands have made me, and fashioned me: instruct me, that I will learn Your commandments. They who fear You shall see me and rejoice: for I have hoped in Your words. I know, O Lord, that Your judgments are righteousness, and that You truly have humbled me. Let, Your mercy come upon me to comfort me, according to Your word to Your servant. Let Your compassion come to me, that I shall live: for Your law is my meditation. Let the proud be ashamed: for they transgressed against me unjustly: but I shall be continually in Your commandments. Let those who fear You, and those who know Your wonders, turn to me. Let my heart be blameless in Your ordinances, that I may not be ashamed. *(Zoxasi..)*

(11) My soul has fainted for Your salvation: and I have hoped in Your words. My eyes failed in waiting for Your word, saying, "When will You comfort me?" I have become as a bottle in the frost: but I have not forgotten Your ordinances. How many are the days of Your servant? When will You execute judgment for me on those who persecute me? Transgressors told me idle words; but not according to Your law, O Lord. For all Your commandments are truth; they persecuted me unjustly; help me. They nearly destroyed me upon the earth; but I did not forsake Your commandments. Revive me according to Your mercy; so I shall keep the testimonies of Your mouth. *(Zoxasi..)*

(12) Your word, O Lord, abides in the heavens forever. Your truth endures from generation to generation; You have founded the earth, and it abides by Your command. The day also abides; for all things are Your servants. Were it not that Your law was my meditation, I would have perished in my humility. I shall never forget Your ordinances; for with them You have revived me. I am Yours, save me; for I have sought out Your ordinances. The sinners have waited for me to destroy me; but I understood Your testimonies. I have seen an end of every perfection; but Your commandments are very broad. *(Zoxasi..)*

(13) How beloved is Your name, O Lord! It is my meditation the whole day. You have instructed me more than my enemies in Your commandments; for they are mine forever. I have more understanding than all who teach me; for Your testimonies are my meditation. I understood more than the aged; because I sought out Your commandments. I have kept back my feet from every evil way, that I might keep Your words. I have not declined from Your judgments; for You have set a law for me. How sweet are Your words to my throat, more so than honey and honey comb in my mouth! I gain understanding from Your commandments: therefore I have hated every way of unrighteousness, for You have set a law for me. *(Zoxasi..)*

(14) Your law is a lamp to my feet, and a light to my paths. I have sworn and determined to keep the judgments of Your righteousness. I have been greatly humbled, revive me, O Lord, according to Your word. Bless, O Lord, the promises of my mouth, and teach me Your judgments. My soul is continually in Your hands; and I have not forgotten Your law. The sinners hid a snare for me; and I did not stray from Your commandments. I have inherited Your testimonies forever; for they are the joy of my heart. I have inclined my heart to perform Your righteousness forever, for the sake of a reward. *(Zoxasi..)*

(15) I have hated transgressors; and I have loved Your law. You are my helper and my supporter; I have hoped in Your word. Turn away from me, you evil-doers; for I shall search out the commandments of my God. Uphold me according to Your word, and I shall live; and do not make me ashamed of my hope. Help me, and I shall be saved; and I shall meditate on Your ordinances continually. You have brought to nought all who turn away from Your ordinances; for their thought is an iniquity. I have reckoned all the sinners of the earth as transgressors; therefore I have loved Your testimonies at all times. Nail Your fear to my flesh; for I feared Your judgments. *(Zoxasi..)*

(16) I have done judgment and justice; do not deliver me to the hands of those who injure me. Accept Your servant unto You for good: do not let the proud say falsehood against me. My eyes have failed for Your salvation, and for the word of Your righteousness. Deal with Your servant according to Your mercy, and teach me Your ordinances. I am Your servant; instruct me, and I will know Your testimonies. It is the time to work for the Lord: they have utterly broken Your law. Therefore I have loved Your commandments more than gold and topaz. Therefore I stood for all Your commandments: I have hated every unjust way. *(Zoxasi..)*

(17) Your testimonies are wonderful: therefore my soul has kept them. The manifestation of Your words shall enlighten, and instruct the small children. I opened my mouth, and drew a spirit unto me: for I earnestly longed for Your commandments. Look upon me and have mercy on me, after the manner of those who love Your name. Make straight my steps according to Your word: and let not any iniquity have dominion over me. Deliver me from the false accusation of men: so I shall keep Your commandments. Let Your face shine upon Your servant: and teach me Your ordinances. My eyes have been bathed in the streams of waters, because they did not keep Your law. *(Zoxasi..)*

(18) Righteous are You, O Lord, and upright are Your judgments. You have commanded justice and truth exceedingly, which are Your testimonies. The zeal has eaten me up: because my enemies have forgotten Your commandments. Your word has been very fully tried; and Your servant loves it. I am young and despised: yet I have not forgotten Your ordinances. Your righteousness is an everlasting righteousness, and Your word is truth. Afflictions and distresses found me: but Your commandments are my meditation. Your testimonies are righteousness forever: instruct me, and I shall live. *(Zoxasi..)*

(19) I cried with my whole heart; hear me, O Lord: I shall search out Your ordinances. I cried up to You; save me, and I shall keep Your testimonies. I hastened to arise before the time, and cried: and I hoped in Your word. My eyes hastened to awake before the dawn, that I might meditate on Your words. Hear my voice, O Lord, according to Your mercy; revive me according to Your judgments. They have drawn near who persecuted me in iniquity; and they are far removed from Your law. You are near, O Lord; and all Your commandments are truth. Since the beginning I knew from Your testimonies, that You had founded them forever. *(Zoxasi..)*

(20) Look upon my humiliation, and save me: for I have not forgotten Your law. Plead my cause, and redeem me: revive me for the sake of Your word. Salvation is far from sinners: for they have not searched out Your ordinances. Your mercies, O Lord, are many: revive me according to Your judgments. Many are they who persecute me and distress me: but I did not turn away from Your testimonies. I beheld foolish men, and I suffered; for they did not keep Your words. Behold, O Lord, I have loved Your commandments: revive me in Your mercy. The beginning of Your words is truth; and all judgments of Your righteousness are forever. *(Zoxasi..)*

(21) Princes persecuted me without a cause, my heart was afraid of Your words. I will exult because of Your words, as one who has found a great treasure. I hated and abhorred unrighteousness; but I loved Your law. Seven times a day I have praised You because of the judgments of Your righteousness. Let great peace be for those who love Your law: and there is no stumbling in them. I waited for Your salvation, O Lord, and have loved Your commandments. My soul has kept Your testimonies, and loved them exceedingly. I have kept Your commandments and Your testimonies; and all my ways are before You, O Lord. *(Zoxasi..)*

(22) Let my supplication come near before You; give me understanding according to Your word. Let my petition come before You, revive me according to Your word. Let my lips flow with praise, when You have taught me Your ordinances. Let my tongue speak of Your words; for all Your commandments are righteous. Let Your hand be for saving me; for I have desired Your commandments. I have longed for Your salvation, O Lord; and Your law is my meditation. My soul shall live and praise You; and Your judgments shall help me. I have gone astray like a lost sheep; seek Your servant; for I have not forgotten Your commandments. **Alleluia.**

THE HOLY GOSPEL ACCORDING TO ST. MATTHEW (CH. 25:1-13)

Then the kingdom of heaven shall be likened to ten virgins, who took their lamps, and went forth to meet the bridegroom. And five of them were wise, and five were foolish. Those who were foolish took their lamps, and took no oil with them: But the wise took oil in their vessels with their lamps. While the bridegroom was delayed, they all slumbered and slept. And at midnight there was a cry made, "Behold, the bridegroom is coming; go out to meet him." Then all those virgins arose, and trimmed their lamps. And the foolish said unto the wise, "Give us of your oil; for our lamps are going out." But the wise answered, saying, "No; lest there should not be enough for us and you: but go rather to those who sell, and buy for yourselves." And while they went to buy, the bridegroom came; and those who were ready went in with him to the marriage: and the door was shut. Afterward the other virgins came also, saying, "Lord, Lord, open to us." But he answered and said, "Verily I say unto you, I do not know you." Watch therefore, for you know neither the day nor the hour in which the Son of Man is coming. Glory to God forever. Amen.

LITANIES

(1) Behold, the Bridegroom is coming at midnight, blessed is the servant whom He finds watching. But he whom He finds sleeping is unworthy of going with Him. Therefore, take heed, O my soul, that you may not fall into deep sleep, and then be cast out of the Kingdom. But watch and cry out saying "Holy, Holy, Holy are You, O God; for the sake of the *Theotokos*, have mercy on us." *(Doxa Patri ke Eio ke Agio Pnevmati)*

(2) O my soul, be mindful of that awesome day, and wake up and light your lamp with the oil of joy, for you do not know when the voice will call upon you saying: "Behold, the Bridegroom is coming." So, take heed, my soul, not to fall asleep, lest you stand outside knocking like the five foolish virgins. But watch, entreating that you may meet Christ the Lord with rich oil, and

He may grant you the wedding of His true and heavenly glory. *(Ke nin ke a e ke estos e onas ton e onon amin.)*

(3) You are the rampart of our salvation, O *Theotokos* the Virgin, the mighty and impregnable fortress. Abolish the counsel of the adversaries, and transform the sorrow of your servants into joy. Fortify our city, defend our governors, and intercede for the peace of the world; for you are our hope, O *Theotokos*. *(Ke nin ke a e ke estos e onas ton e onon amin.)*

O Heavenly King...   **page 98**
Kyrie eleison, Lord have mercy (41 times)
HOLY HOLY HOLY   **page 64**
Our Father who art in Heaven...

Midnight Prayer – Second Watch

The praise of the Second Watch of the blessed Midnight Hour, we offer unto Christ our King and our God, beseeching Him to forgive us our sins.

From the Psalms of our father David the prophet and the king, may his blessings be upon us all. Amen.

The Psalms of the Eleventh Hour are prayed, except the first two psalms, psalms 116 and 117, page 170

THE HOLY GOSPEL ACCORDING TO ST. LUKE (CH. 7 : 36-50)

Then one of the Pharisees asked Him to eat with him. And He went unto the Pharisee's house, and sat down to eat. And, behold, a woman in the city, who was a sinner, when she knew that Jesus sat to eat in the Pharisee's house, brought an alabaster box of ointment, and stood at His feet behind Him weeping, and began to wash His feet with tears, and wiped them with the hairs of her head, and kissed His feet, and anointed them with the ointment. Now when the Pharisee who had invited Him saw this, he spoke within himself, saying "This man, if He were a prophet, would have known who and what manner of woman this is who touch Him: for she is a sinner." And Jesus answered and said to him, "Simon, I have something to say to you." And he said, "Master, say it." "There was a certain creditor who had two debtors: one owed five hundred denarii, and the other fifty. And when they had nothing to pay, he freely forgave them both. Tell me therefore, which of them will love him more?" Simon answered and said, "I suppose that he, to whom he forgave more." And He said unto him, "You have rightly judged." And He turned to the woman, and said unto Simon, "Do you see this woman? I entered into your house, you gave Me no water for My feet: but she has washed My feet with tears, and wiped them with the hairs of her head. You gave Me no kiss: but this woman since the time I came in has not ceased to kiss My feet. My head with oil you did not anoint: but this woman has anointed My feet with ointment. Therefore I say unto you, `Her sins, which are many, are forgiven; for she loved much: but to whom little is forgiven, the same loves little."

And He said unto her, "Your sins are forgiven." And they who sat to eat with Him began to say within themselves, "Who is this who forgives sins also?" And He said to the woman, "Your faith has saved you; go in peace."
Glory to God forever. Amen.

LITANIES

(1) Give me, O Lord, many fountains of tears, as You gave, in the past, the sinful woman. Make me worthy to wash Your Feet which liberated me from the path of straying, and to offer you a precious fragrant oil, and gain, through repentance, a pure life, so that I may hear that voice full of joy: "Your faith has saved you." *(Doxa Patri ke Eioa ke Agio Pnevmati)*

(2) When I realize my many wicked deeds, and the thought of that awesome judgment comes to my heart, a tremble takes hold of me, and I take refuge in You, O God, the Lover of mankind. So do not turn away Your face from me, I entreat You, Who alone are without sin. Grant humbleness to my poor soul before the end comes, and save me. *(Ke nin ke a e ke estos e onas ton e onon amin.)*

(3) The Heavens bless you, O full of grace, the Bride who was never married. And we, too, glorify your incomprehensible giving birth. O *Theotokos*, the mother of mercy and salvation, intercede for the salvation of our souls. *(Ke nin ke a e ke estos e onas ton e onon amin.)*

O Heavenly King...   **page 98**
     Kyrie eleison, Lord have mercy (41 times)
HOLY HOLY HOLY   **page 64**
     Our Father who art in Heaven...

Midnight Prayer – Third Watch

The praise of the Third Watch of the blessed Midnight Hour, we offer unto Christ our King and our God, beseeching Him to forgive us our sins.

From the Psalms of our father David the prophet and the king, may his blessings be upon us all. Amen.

The Psalms of the Twelfth Hour are prayed, page 196

THE HOLY GOSPEL ACCORDING TO ST. LUKE (CH 12 : 32-64)

"Do not fear, little flock; for it is your Father's good pleasure to give you the kingdom. Sell what you have, and give alms, provide yourselves money bags which do not grow old, a treasure in the heavens that does not fails, where no thief approaches, nor moth corrupts. For where your treasure is, there your heart will be also. Let your loins be girded, and your lamps burning; And you yourselves be like men who wait for their master, when he will return from the wedding; that when he comes and knocks, they may open to him immediately. Blessed are those servants, whom their master, when he comes will find them: Assuredly I say to you, that he shall gird himself, and have them sit down to eat, and will come and serve them. And if he shall come in the second watch, or come in the third watch, and finds them so, blessed are those servants. But know this, that if the master of the house had known what hour the thief would come, he would have watched, and not have allowed his house to be broken into. You therefore be ready also: for the Son of Man is coming at an hour when you do not think." Then Peter said to Him, "Lord, do you speak this parable only to us, or to all people?" And the Lord said, "Who then is that faithful and wise steward, whom his master will make ruler over his household, to give them their portion of food in due season? Blessed is that servant, whom his master when he comes will find so doing. Truly I say to you, that he will make him ruler over all that he has. But if that servant says in his heart, `My master is delaying his coming;' and begins to beat the menservants and maidens, and to eat and drink, and be drunk; The master of that servant will come in a day when he is not looking for him, and at an hour when he is not aware, and will cut him in two, and appoint him his portion with the unbelievers." Glory to God forever. Amen.

LITANIES

(1) With a compassionate eye, O Lord, look at my weakness, for shortly my life will end, and in my deeds I shall have no salvation. Therefore, I beseech, O Lord, with a merciful eye look at my weakness, my humility, my poverty and my sojourn, and save me. (*Doxa ...*)

(2) As the Judge is present, take heed, O my soul, awake and consider that awesome hour; for in the day of judgment, there will be no mercy on those who were not merciful. Therefore, have compassion on me, O Savior, for You alone are the Lover of mankind. . (*Ke nin ...*)

(3) O the reasonable gate of life, the honored *Theotokos*, deliver from hardships those who, in faith, take refuge in you, so that we might glorify your immaculate birth of Christ for the salvation of our souls. . (*Ke nin ...*)

O Heavenly King...   **page 98**
  Kyrie eleison, Lord have mercy (41 times)
HOLY HOLY HOLY   **page 64**
  Our Father who art in Heaven...

THE HOLY GOSPEL ACCORDING TO ST. LUKE (CH. 2 : 29-32)

Lord, now let your servant depart in peace, according to Your word: For my eyes have seen Your salvation, which You have prepared before the face of people; A light to be revealed to the Gentiles and a glory of Your people Israel. Glory be to God forever. Amen.

INTRODUCTION TO THE CREED page 60
THE ORTHODOX CREED   **page 60**
  Kyrie eleison, Lord have mercy (41 times)
HOLY HOLY HOLY   **page 64**
  Our Father who art in Heaven...

ABSOLUTION

O Lord and Master, Jesus Christ, the Living and Eternal Son of God, enlighten our minds to understand Your life-giving words. Raise us up from the darkness of sin which ruins the soul. Make us worthy to become upright in good deeds. And at the time of Your coming to judge the world, make us worthy of hearing that voice full of joy saying, "Come to Me you blessed of My Father, inherit the Kingdom prepared for you before the foundation of the world." Yes, Lord, grant us in that Hour to be without fear, anxiety or condemnation; and do not judge us according to our many iniquities. For You alone are compassionate, longsuffering and exceedingly merciful. We ask this, through the intercession of our Lady the Theotokos, Saint Mary, and the intercession of all the choir of Your saints. Amen.

THE CONCLUSION OF EVERY HOUR
page 68

Absolution of the Priests

We ask You, O Master Lord Jesus Christ, Son of the Living God, existing in Light before all ages, Light of Light: Enlighten O Lord, our minds and hearts and shine on our understanding, that we may understand your life-giving word. Raise us from darkness of sin that kills the soul. Make us worthy to be upright in doing good and righteousness. At the time of Your awesome second coming to judge the world, make us worthy of hearing the voice full of happiness, gladness, comfort and joy from Your Divine mouth saying, "Come you, blessed of My Father, inherit the kingdom prepared for you from the foundation of the world." Yes, O Lord, help us to be on that day and in that hour without fear or blemish or terror or falling or straying. Do not condemn us, O Lord, for the multitude of our sins. Forgive us, O Lord, all our transgressions, iniquities, mistakes and shortcomings.

Take away from us and from the whole world death, inflation, plagues, destruction, evacuation, the sword of enemies, the conspiracy of devils, the evil of fire and drowning, the fight of evil-doers, the deception of the wicked, and the injustice of the ruler. Abolish from us the conspiracy of those who are opposing us.

O God, You are our Lord and our God; have compassion on us and do not throw us in the seas of destruction or the paths of punishment, but deliver us and keep us and cover us and raise us from our boredom, slothfulness and laziness. Do not let our enemy, the devil, deceive us by false hopes, but alert our minds and wake up our hearts from the sleep of carelessness and wasting life in vain. O God, forsake our sins. Forgive our iniquities. Do not remember our trespasses. Do not get angry with us, and do not let Your anger endure forever. Have mercy on us, O Lord, and have mercy on us, for we are weak and poor and drowning in the sea of sins. We cry unto You; we worship You; we claim You; we entreat You: Do not dash, O Lord, our hope in Your mercy. Do not shut the door of Your mercy in our faces. Graciously save us and lead us to Your mercy. Make us to hear Your joyful voice.

O God, purify us and sanctify our hearts from evil, defiled, and bad thoughts. Abolish from us, O Lord, and from all Your people, all devilish dreams and illusions. Raise us, O God, from every fall and affliction. Confirm in us, O God, patience and hope and love and the orthodox faith. Count us with Your sheep at Your right hand. Set us down with those who sit at Your heavenly banquet. Forgive us every iniquity, trespass and sin. Fortify us with the strength of Your heavenly angels of light, for we have no salvation except through Your grace and our trust and belief and hope in You. Accept from us, O Lord., our supplication at this present time and at all times. All those who have bidden and asked us to remember them in prayers, liturgies, and commemorations, the living and the dead, remember them, along with us, O Lord, for that which is good in the heavenly Jerusalem, in the kingdom of heaven.

Blot out, O Lord, our trespasses. As for those who have trespassed against us, forgive them and us. Through Your mercy, O Lord., save the souls of us all. O Lord, save Your people. Bless Your inheritance. Shepherd them and raise them up forever. Save all those who are in afflictions, tribulations or sorrows. Release those who are captive by the bonds of the devils. Satisfy the hungry with good things. Comfort those who are sad in the heart and soul. Raise the fallen. Confirm the upright. Bring back those who have strayed. Support the widows and orphans. Help the needy. Give blessing to the fruits of the earth, good temper to the air, growth to the trees and full measure to the rivers. Bless dew and rain. Give contentment to the poor. Pay for the debtors. Gather together the dispersed. Accept the repentance of the repentant. Receive the confession of the confessors. Give understanding to the catechumens. Judge, O Lord, for the oppressed.

Fill our hearts with happiness, gladness, comfort and joy that we, having sufficiency in everything, always may abound in good and acceptable deeds. Bless, O Lord, the harvest with Your heavenly blessings. Bless the crown of this year with Your goodness. Bless, O Lord, those who sow and plant and reap, as You blessed for the children of Israel the harvest of the sixth year.

Bless, O Lord, this, our congregation and all congregations of the orthodox people. Keep for us and upon us the life and primacy of our master and father the Patriarch Pope Abba (....), the patriarch of this time; save him, O Lord, and save his people from all afflictions, temptations, and hardships, along with his partners in the apostolic service, our fathers the metropolitans, our fathers the bishops, our fathers the hegumens, our fathers the priests, our brothers the deacons, our fathers the monks and our brethren the laymen. As for those who came now, attending and participating with us in this prayer and all orthodox prayers, asking forgiveness of their sins and mercy for their souls, bless us and bless them; absolve us and absolve them; forgive us and them our sins, in the past and in the future, the personal and impersonal, the sins of the day and sins of the night, the hidden and manifest.

Keep O Lord, the liveliness of holy orthodox congregations, churches and monasteries, and the elders who live in them, and those who are serving them, those who are managing them and those who are dwelling in them. Put security, peace, love and stability among them. Subdue the evil enemy under their feet and our feet. Do not allow him to have any part in them or in us, neither by the left attack or the right attack. Keep them with Your most high hand and strong arm. Deliver us, O my Master, from bad temptations and traps that are set, seen or unseen

Remember, O Lord, our fathers, our mothers, our brethren, our families, our relatives, our teachers, our spiritual and natural children, and all of the children of baptism. Remember, O Lord, those from whom we ate and drank of their effort and labor, and who sheltered us in their houses and gave us from their hands. Reward them, O Lord, and give them the incorruptible instead of the corruptible, the heavenly instead of the earthly. Fill their houses and stores with all good things. Reward them, O Lord, thirty-fold, sixty-fold and a hundred-fold, along with the forgiveness of their sins in the kingdom of heaven. Remember O Lord, those who give alms to us or to our brethren the needy in all forms of charity, for loving You and honoring Your holy name; bless them.

Remember, O Lord, those who care for the sacrifices, oblations, donations, wine, oil, first-fruits, incense, coverings, vows, books and all altar vessels; reward them O Lord, for their gifts by the forgiveness of their sins. Grant them the happy life in this present age, and the eternal life in the age to come.

Remember, O Lord, our fathers and brethren who have already fallen asleep and reposed in the right faith, repose O, Lord, all their souls in the bosoms of our fathers, Abraham, Isaac and Jacob, in the region of the living, in the heavenly Jerusalem. As for us, the living, help us for the salvation of our souls. Manage our lives according to Your good will.

Graciously, O Lord, remember my abject self, my poverty, and my weakness. 1, the sinner and miserable, who is not worthy to stand in Your presence for the multitude of my sins and iniquities, do not reject me. Raise, O Lord, a horn of salvation for your people by the sign of Your life-giving cross. Grant O Lord, Your relief during tribulations, Your help during hardships and disasters. Save us, O Lord, and save all those who are in distress. Heal the sick of Your people. Make, O Lord, Your Christian people, those who are present with us, and those who are absent, to be blessed and absolved from Your divine mouth, from the rising of the sun to its setting, and from the north to the south Accept us unto You, as You accepted the thief on the right hand while You were on the tree of the cross, and granted him the paradise of joy.

Remember, O Lord, the orphans, the widows, the isolated, the handicapped, and those who have no one to mention them; remember them and us, O Lord, in the heavenly Jerusalem. Remember O Lord, those who are standing up or sitting down, or laying down or ejected; those who are traveling by land, sea or air, in rough or smooth ways, in valleys, roadways, mountaintops, hills or caves, those who are in dungeons or prisons, and those who are in exile or captivity, and those who are held in the bondage of authorities and devils; deliver them. Bring them back and get them all into the haven, safe, winners, satisfied, and healthy in soul, body and spirit.

Grant, My Lord Jesus Christ, that this, our prayer, be acceptable to You, without hypocrisy, pride, haughtiness or blemish. Help us, O God, to please You. Help us to follow Your commandments. Help us to encounter the pangs of death, before death and after death, for You are good God, long-suffering and abundant in mercy and compassion. O God, make the door of Your church to be open for us through the ages and until the end of all ages.

Have mercy on us, O God, according to Your great mercy, through the great intercessor, the source of purity, generosity and blessedness, the lady of us all, the pride of our race, the virgin, the chosen St. Mary, the honorable martyr St. Mark, the evangelist, the apostle and the preacher of the land of Egypt, and all angels, patriarchs, prophets, apostles, martyrs, saints, anchorites, worshippers, hermits, strivers and those who pleased You by their good deeds, from Adam to the end of ages.

We worship You, O Holy Trinity, the Father, and the Son and the Holy Spirit, now and forever and unto the ages of all ages. Amen.

Make us worthy to pray thankfully: **Our Father Who art in heaven ...**

Prayer for Repentance

My Lord, God and Savior Jesus Christ, the treasury of mercy and fountain of salvation, I come to You confessing my sins. I confess that with boldness I dared to defile Your holy sanctuary with my many sins. Now, I resort to Your tender mercy and compassion, for Your mercy is immeasurable. You have not rejected any sinner; accept me to You. Behold, O Lord, I come confessing that my sins have piled upon my head as a heavy burden. I have no strength.

Do not hide Your face from me lest I become afraid. Do not rebuke me in Your anger, O Lord, nor chasten me in Your wrath. Do not judge me according to my sins. Have mercy on me O Lord, for I am weak. Remember O Lord, that I am Your handiwork; have pity on me. Do not enter into judgment with Your servant, for in Your sight no one living shall be justified. Come and clothe me again with a new garment suitable for Your glory. Forgive me and absolve me that I may sing to You saying, "Blessed is he whose transgression is forgiven and whose sins are covered. I confess my sins to You, and do not hide my iniquity. I said that I will confess my transgressions to You Oh Lord, and You will forgive the iniquity of my sin." Glory be to You forever. Amen.

Prayer before Confession

My Holy Father, Who delights in the repentance of sinners, You promised that You are ready to accept them. Look now, my Lord, upon a sinning soul which went astray in valleys of rebellion for a long time, in which it was embittered and felt its misery, estranged from the Fountain of its salvation. Now I proceed to You asking You for its purification from the filthiness and mud in which it was wallowing. Accept it and do not reject it, for if You look at it in Your kindness and deal with it in Your tender mercy, it will be purified and saved, and if You ignore it, it will perish and fall into perdition. Grant me, O Lord, a grace by which I dare approach You with strong faith and complete and perfect hope in order to confess my iniquities and hate to return to them. Let Your Spirit rebuke me for my sins. Enlighten my heart to recognize how much I have sinned, transgressed, missed, and broken Your commandments, and how many times I failed to do those things You would have me do.

Grant me Oh Lord, to determine not to return to sin in order to dwell in You and keep Your commandments so that I may live for glorifying Your Holy Name. Amen.

Prayer after Confession

I thank Your goodness, O Father the Lover of Mankind, for You did not wish that I should perish, but You wakened me from my forgetfulness, guided me into Your way, and restored me from the valley of perdition into the refuge of Your safe fortress. Fill me with hope and faith. I proceeded unto You O Lord, like a patient who comes to the healing physician, and like the hungry to life-sustaining food, and like the thirsty to the springs of living water and like the poor to the source of richness, and like the sinner to the Savior, and like the dead to the fountain of life. You are my salvation, my physician, my strength, my comfort, and my happiness. In You is my rest, so help me and guard me. Encompass me and teach me to put all my will in Your hands and walk according to what You wish. Help my weakness that I may dwell and be steadfast and continue to be faithful to You unto the end. Amen.

Prayer before Communion

O Lord, Master Jesus Christ, the Prince of Life and the King of Ages, the Bread of Life which came down from heaven, Who granted life to those who partake of Your holy body and precious blood, grant Your servant Your heavenly blessings in order to be worthy to approach the mystery of Your holy body and blood in godliness and reverence. Wake my heart to Your grace and visit me with Your salvation that I may taste the sweetness of Your heavenly grace hidden entirely in this all-holy mystery. Grant me a strong faith far from doubt and skepticism, that I may approach You now, trusting that this is Your holy body and precious blood, O Emmanuel, our God. Make me worthy to partake of them without falling into condemnation, in order to be united with You spiritually and for the forgiveness of my sins and for acceptance before Your awful judgment: for Yours is the glory with Your good Father and the Holy Spirit, now and forever. Amen.

Prayer after Communion

How great is Your generosity, O God, which You prepared for those who fear You! How sweet is Your grace and love for those who love You! I thank You, my Lord, Who cares for me and gave me this holy, mysterious and everlasting food by which You open for us the way to eternal life. Keep me under the shadow of Your wings, and grant that, with a pure conscience, even until my last breath, I may worthily partake of Your holy things, for the remission of my sins and for life eternal. Enflame in me the fire of Your love, and keep the gift of Your grace in me, neither for judgment nor for falling into condemnation, but for gaining glory and purity of soul and body in order to live in You and for You. Guide me into Your righteousness. Fill my heart with Your grace. Sanctify my life with Your Holy Spirit, for Yours is the glory with Your gracious Father and the Holy Spirit, now and forever. Amen.

Prayer Asking for the Will of God

My God, You know that I do not know what is good for me. Behold, I am thinking of ……... How can I know what is good and useful for me if

You do not guide me through Your grace?! Therefore, I ask You, my Lord, to guide me concerning Your will about this matter. Do not leave me to my own counsel, following only my own desires, lest I get in trouble and, fall. Keep Your servant from falling, and be my support and help. Manage the matter according to Your will as it pleases Your goodness. If it is good in Your eyes, let it be according to Your will, and give me Your grace to accomplish it. If it would hurt, please take from me this aim, for You are All-knowing. Nothing is hidden from You. I am Your servant, O Lord. Deal with me according to what You deem fit, for there is no complete success or perfect peace without submitting myself to the guidance of Your will. Teach me to say in everything, "My Father let it be not according to my will, but let Your will be done. " For Yours is the kingdom, and the power, and the glory forever. Amen

Prayer before Eating

Blessed are You O Lord, Who supports us from our birth, and grants us Your blessings. You prepares food for every creature; for the eyes of all hope in You, for You give them their food in due season. You open Your hands and satisfy every living creature by Your goodness. To You is due glory, praise, blessing and thanksgiving for the food that You have prepared for us. Stretch forth Your right hand and bless this food set before us for the nourishment of our bodies. Let it be for the power and health of our lives. Grant salvation, grace, blessing and purity to all those who partake thereof. Lift our minds to You at all times to seek our spiritual and eternal food. Grant that we may labor for the everlasting food which is for eternal life. Grant us to be partakers of Your evening banquet. Give us the food of blessing, the cup of salvation, and fill our hearts with joy. Grant us a peaceful life, joy of the soul, and health of the body. Teach us to seek your pleasure in all things so that when eating, drinking, or laboring, we do it all for the glory of Your Holy Name. For Yours is the glory forever and ever. Amen.

Make us worthy to pray thankfully: **Our Father Who art in heaven ...**

Prayer from the Psalmody

O our Lord Jesus Christ, who carries the sin of the world, count us with Your sheep, those who are to Your right. And when You come again in Your second fearful appearance, may we never fearfully hear You say, "I do not know you." But rather may we be made worthy to hear the voice, full of joy, of Your tender mercies, proclaiming and saying, "Come unto Me, O blessed of My Father, and inherit the life that endures forever."

The martyrs will come, bearing their afflictions, and the righteous will come, bearing their virtues. The Son of God shall come in His glory, and His Father's glory, to give unto everyone according to his deeds which he has done.

O Christ, the Word of the Father, the Only Begotten God, grant us Your peace that is full of joy. As You have given to Your saintly apostles, likewise also say to us, "My peace I give unto you. My peace which I have taken from My Father, I leave unto you, both now and forever."

O the angel of this day, flying up with this hymn, remember us before the Lord, that He may forgive us our sins. The sick heal them. Those who have slept, O Lord, repose them, and all of our brothers in distress, help us my Lord, and all of them. May God bless us, and let us bless His Holy Name, and may His praise continually be upon our mouths. Blessed is the Father and the Son, and the Holy Spirit, the perfect Trinity, we worship and glorify Him.

Make us worthy to pray thankfully: **Our Father Who art in heaven ...**

Made in the USA
Columbia, SC
09 March 2023

13574207R00102